— *PRAISE FOR* —
Not Always Home Before Dark

"...*More than a dog book, it is a love story, a book that goes to the heart of the long, tangled relationship between dogs and humans, and most of all a terrific read even for people who don't want a large dog in their life. Cajun, Brooke Newman's rescue dog, comes across as a real, complicated, fascinating, infuriating character, and the story of his life with Brooke (or hers with him) will bring laughter, happiness and tears to even the most confirmed dogophobic. Elegantly written, beautifully observed, great fun, it is that rarest of things, a book that will make you feel better about life—and about dogs and people.*"

Michael Korda, author of *Passing*

ALSO BY
Brooke Newman

The Little Tern
JennieMae and James
Issues and Trends in Health
The Lost Tern
My Mother's Lovers

— Not Always — Home Before Dark

From the French Quarter of New Orleans
to the ski slopes of Aspen to the Oceanside of Truro
to the cornfields of Iowa City and the truck stops of Omaha...

Brooke Newman

Book design by Jessika Hazelton
Printed in the United States of America
The Troy Book Makers • Troy, New York • thetroybookmakers.com

To order additional copies of this title,
contact your favorite local bookstore
or visit www.shoptbmbooks.com

Paperback ISBN: 978-1-61468-571-5
Hardcover ISBN: 978-1-61468-572-2

"The world breaks everyone, and afterward, some are strong at the broken places."

—Ernest Hemingway

FOR CAJUN

And for Nikos, Blue, Joe
And for my grandchildren
And for Mark

contents

PREFACE

The unthinkable

Hurricane Katrina hit the southeastern coast of Louisiana on the morning of August 29, 2005, making landfall near Buras-Triumph with sustained winds measuring 125 mph. It was a morning that would not easily be forgotten in New Orleans as an immense storm surge with tides in excess of 14 feet, coupled with an inundating rainfall as high as 15 inches flooded Lake Pontchartrain and overflowed into St Tammany, Tangipahoa, St John the Baptist and St Charles parishes. Levees that were supposed to protect the city were breached and 80% of the city was flooded.

Windows were blown out of buildings and houses, bridges collapsed, highways, byways, alleys, and roads were flooded, and those roads that were not flooded were so severely damaged they were impassable. Barges and boats were picked up as if they were toothpicks and thrown onto dry land. Quite a number of structures were lifted from their foundations and relocated wherever the waters took them. The sounds within the city and surrounding areas were described as "sounds from hell" as the winds howled and the rain pelted the landscape, and as sirens roared and rescue helicopter rotors fluttered. Survival soon became the only thing on everyone's mind. People quickly gathered their most cherished belongings and brought them along as they searched for a safe place. 26,000 people packed into the Superdome, while alternative accommodations were created by the Red Cross and other organizations wherever it was possible.

However, pets were not allowed in almost any of these places.

It has been estimated that as many as 250,000 animals were left behind or stranded following Hurricane Katrina. In New Orleans alone it was estimated that at least 50,000 dogs and cats were abandoned, though not by choice since some families thought they would be returning home soon and left their pets "temporarily", while others were told by various authorities that they could not bring a pet into housing spaces, such as the Louisiana Superdome, and they were therefore forced to leave their pets behind, and still others simply did not know what to do and just left their pets behind. Soon after the hurricane hit numerous animal groups organized both nationally and locally to create rescue operations and shelters to care for the animals. Within twenty-four hours of the storm, the Humane Society immediately began to organize animal relief efforts. They designated the Lamar-Dixon Equine Expo Center as the center for these efforts and approximately 10,000 animals were brought there. Veterinarians, veterinarian technicians and volunteers from far and wide worked at Lamar-Dixon in some of the most difficult and trying conditions.

The humidity was oppressive, the temperature often rose above 100 degrees, mosquitoes were ubiquitous, trash removal and clean-up efforts were exceedingly difficult, fatigue levels were always high, confusion over which animals needed what medication, when, and how often was commonplace.

According to Dr. Karen Halligan, who was the Director of Veterinary Services, SPCA:LA, "the ma-

jority of animals coming in were underweight, dehy-
drated and covered in dry sludge with a distinct odor.
There were dogs with scabies, parvo, bite wounds,
fungal infections and hyperthermia... one VMAT estimated that 60 to 80 percent of the rescued animals
most likely had or would develop heartworm."

Dr. Halligan went on to say that "more than
15,000 animals in the area were ultimately rescued
by humane organizations. Of those that were rescued, only 15 to 20 percent were ever reunited with
their owners. The number of animals that died during Hurricane Katrina due to drowning, starvation,
disease and misfortune is unknown, but is thought to
be in the tens of thousands."

CHAPTER ONE

The "One"

*"Unless someone like you cares a whole awful lot,
nothing is going to get better.
It's not."* —Dr. Seuss

If you are a person who grew up with dogs, and always
had at least one or two or three by your side, you will
understand that oftentimes there is one who captured
your heart and soul more than any other. The mal-
nourished, mistreated, and sickly dog I adopted after
Hurricane Katrina was that "one" for me, and little did
he know that after being rescued in New Orleans he

would live a more or less globe-trotting life, annually traveling from Aspen, Colorado to Truro, Massachusetts and experiencing adventures along the way in the corn-fields of Iowa, the motels of Nebraska and Indiana, the farm fields of Ohio, the rest stops of Pennsylvania and the state patrol arrests in New York.

Over the years, I have adopted, purchased, found, been left with Newfoundlands, Golden Retrievers, Border Collies, Great Pyrenees, Dachshunds, Labrador Retrievers, Shelties, Boxers, and mutts. And I have loved them all. But there was this one. And there will never be another like him. He and I connected in a way that was singular and exceptional, and just damn special. A mutt who had been found wandering the flooded and filthy streets of St. Bernard Parish during the aftermath of Hurricane Katrina. I fostered and then adopted him, named him Cajun, and spent the next fifteen years with the most engaging, inimitable, thoroughly unique, exhausting, unconventional best friend a person could ever have. Known and photographed by thousands—literally worldwide—as "the wedding crasher", the "uninvited party guest", the wanderer, the Harbor Mayor, the lover and then leaver, the independent and carefree rover who knew just when he wanted to return home and when he would return home, the sweet yellow dog with the perceptive and sage eyes, the dog understandably sent into spasms of fear and shaking by a clap of thunder heard seventy-five miles in the distance or by wind gusts over twenty miles an hour or by lightening or heavy downpours or fireworks or any loud noise, the dog who never barked, never scratched on a door, never made any demands except to be appreciated and loved for who he was. And I did that because he deserved it. From the first day I laid eyes upon him in that cage, in the shelter. He was a gift. The best friend I will ever have…and for which I am forever thankful.

This story is about love. It is about Cajun.

CHAPTER TWO

Lend a Hand, Have a Heart

Early on the morning of September 9th—eleven days after Hurricane Katrina had devastated New Orleans—my telephone rang. It was Seth Sachson, the Director of the Aspen Animal Shelter calling to say that the two women (Anne Gurchick and Bland Nesbit) who had flown to New Orleans to help in animal rescue efforts had just arrived back in town with 20 very needy dogs, and all of these dogs needed foster homes.

"We have some very frightened dogs out here that need care. Would you consider fostering one?" Seth asked.

"Well...sure...I suppose so...when did they arrive?" I hesitated for only a moment.

"About an hour ago."

"Okay. I'll be right out," I told him, and then spun around to quickly inform Mark—my rational and empathetic "significant other"—what "we" were thinking about doing...since I had not yet mentioned what had already been set in motion.

However, when it came to the decision of whether or not to foster a dog I was fairly confident that Mark wasn't likely to disagree since he too is a dog person—though he is one who believes that caring for one dog would be perfect, caring for two is within the realm of reason, but more than two would be ludicrous—and we already had two dogs.

So with this new possible twist affecting our household, Mark was skeptical but he too had

watched as the reports came in about Hurricane Katrina and wanted to aid in whatever way we could.

Mark raised his thick black eyebrows, threw both
hands in the air and minutes later we were in the
driveway loading our two dogs into my truck: one
a very large 150-pound, black, sweet two year old
female Newfoundland who was big enough to count
as two dogs, and the other a five-yearold black and
tan miniature long-haired dachshund who was small
and feisty enough to account for more than herself.

The Newfoundland became part of our family
because we had owned one of these gentle giants
before and took to their loving, loyal nature. The
Dachshund I adopted when my oldest son begged
me to take his then-girlfriend's puppy, since when
they moved in together his allergies and the puppy
were not compatible.

So, since I am a well-known sucker for stray
dogs, injured birds, turtles, bunnies, and chipmunks,
along with being the "go-to" person for my children's
sometimes unwise or ill thought-out decisions, I have
frequently ended up with more than one dog in the
house, three horses, turtles, numerous gerbils and
hamsters, two cockatiels, and four bunnies.

I also have been known to spend more money on pet food and veterinary bills and dog medications than I have on my human family, much to their chagrin and friendly chiding. And, I am widely known to have vowed more than a dozen times that one day in the very near future I will have only one dog; however, not only do my children roll their eyes when I say this, so too is this the reaction from Mark, my neighbors and friends.

CHAPTER THREE

Draft Pick

Mark has worked in hockey on a professional level for most of his adult life as a coach, a General Manager, and an instructor, and will quickly point out that the dog we took home that morning was not a first round draft pick. However, that isn't entirely true: when we arrived at the shelter and walked down the hall lined with cages of desperate, dirty, unhealthy, anxious, and forlorn barking dogs, I was quickly drawn to one frantic mess of a mutt.

This particular dog was yellow, about the size of a lab, with a very thick neck; I immediately noticed that his chestnut brown eyes darted frantically from spot to spot, person to person, dog to dog. He was so thin that his ribs protruded from his sides, his coat was matted with clumps of what looked like dirt (or was it dried blood?), and he had a scar below his right eye, sores running down his hind legs, and a spiked collar.

While most of the other dogs in separate kennels were either standing or sitting as they barked and howled, the yellow dog was not barking. He didn't make a sound—he didn't bark, he didn't howl, and he didn't yelp. Nor was he standing or sitting—he voiced his pleadings in a different way. He made himself seen rather than heard, and did this by throwing himself against the cage, jumping and pawing at it, and then retreating a few feet where he would spin in a few circles before again throwing himself against the wired kennel. He repeated this routine again and again without ever once letting out so much as a groan. This obsessed dog was unnerved and determined to get out of this situation.

I stopped in front of his kennel and knelt down to offer some soothing words, but my attempts were drowned out by the yelps of the other dogs.

Apprehensively, the yellow dog looked at me, and for just a moment ceased his frenetic behavior. I leaned in against the cage and tried to reassure him that all would soon be fine. He cocked his head.

"It's okay," I told him. "You're going to be okay now."

I turned toward Mark and said, "Let's take this guy. Let's take him."

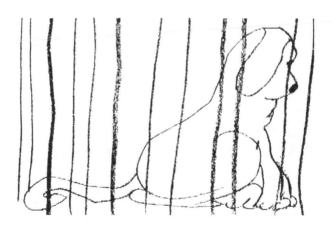

"You haven't even looked at the other dogs," Mark replied. "He's too big. We already have a big dog. Let's find a smaller one." Mark is a rational man. He is almost always calm, collected, considered, and considerate. Very little rattles him, unlike me who tends toward the passionate and emotional and irrational.

Two hours later, having looked at and taken walks with a few other dogs, I convinced Mark that the yellow dog was "the one". Because he was a Katrina dog and there was a chance his family was searching for him, we had to acknowledge that we would foster this rescued dog for up to 18 months. If after 18 months he was not found through Petfinder.com or any other source, then we would have the option of adopting him.

Once the paperwork and veterinarian examination was complete (the dog had ear infections, and also needed to be neutered and treated for a severe case of heartworm— a potentially fatal parasitic disease contracted by dogs through mosquitoes) we were on our way home with three dogs in the truck.

When we arrived home it was obvious that the first order of business was giving this filthy, rank dog a bath.

Three baths later the yellow dog looked and smelled just fine, his spiked collar was replaced for a simple blue nylon one, and our next task lay ahead. He had to have a name.

What's in a dog's name anyway? It's a people thing—a moniker—but it carries some significance (at least the people think it does). How a dog ends up with a name is all about the owner. Most dogs are lucky enough to get one name for life, but then there are those abandoned or rescued dogs who through some circumstance or another have lost their identification; these dogs get a new name.

So here we were with a confused, clean, thin, ailing yellow dog with a new blue nylon collar, and we didn't know how old he was (the veterinarian had estimated in the vicinity of two) and therefore didn't know how long he might have lived with the name Ruffy or Leonard or whatever he was called while living in New Orleans.

No matter what his previous name had been, he needed a new one, and he had no say in the matter. I put it on Mark's shoulders since he's good with things like this, and it didn't take long before he'd come up with a name.

"Cajun. How about the name Cajun?" Mark suggested. "Cajun? Perfect. Cajun it is." And so it was—the yellow dog with the brown spiked collar from somewhere in New Orleans had just been christened Cajun.

CHAPTER FOUR

A Troubled Dog

It didn't take long before it was more than evident that Cajun was a piece of work. He was a mental mess: he had serious issues with loud noises, he had severe abandonment issues, and he had a need for absolute routine that had to be religiously followed. His fear of loud noises was excessive; he wasn't simply frightened by them—he was terrified. At the first hint of a thunderstorm he would shake uncontrollably.

Since he could pick up on the slightest resonance of thunder that might be emanating from over a hundred miles away, a sound inaudible to us was loud and clear to him. If the wind began to blow beyond a meager breeze, his ears would perk up, his eyes would fill with fright, and he would begin to pace and pant. And if there were an impending storm and the skies began to darken, and lightning bolts suddenly lit up the skies, or if tree limbs snapped or cracked, then this poor dog would became inconsolable.

Panting, drooling, and wide-eyed with terror, he would run from room to room to try to find safety. A thunderstorm, firecrackers or fireworks, a gunshot, a car or truck or motorcycle backfiring, dynamite exploding (a common occurrence in a town such as Aspen with four ski mountains, where blasting for avalanche control is frequent), detonations occurring at construction sites, a low-flying jet or helicopter (also common in Aspen when medical emergencies necessitate), blaring music, the honking of a horn—all could and did set Cajun in disarray.

In addition to all of the above, Cajun suffered from severe abandonment issues. He was never able to be convinced that my leaving, if only for a moment, meant being left only for a moment and not forever. Cajun lived in the present, and the second I left his sight or space, he feared he would never see me again.

Yet, curiously and ironically, Cajun had no problem whatsoever with wandering off on his own terms and with his own time schedule in mind. The first couple of years I was privileged enough to be with Cajun he wandered all the time, seemingly searching for something he couldn't find.

I spent more hours than could possibly be logged in any one ledger trying to find him. I drove miles and miles and miles searching for him—hiked, biked, called, bought whistles, searched in the early morning hours before the sun had risen and into the dark hours of the night. And on the occasions I couldn't find him, I would pace and pace until finally he would—and did—return home.

It was my problem, not his. He knew where his home was, but he simply didn't see the need to be there all the time.

There were numerous times I was told about Cajun's adventures while in line at the grocery store—or at the post office, the dry cleaners, the drug store, the school auditorium, the movie theater, or who knew when or where.

My dog Cajun had met hundreds of people at no-one-could-count-how-many locations. He had wandered into houses when doors were left ajar, and walked into schools and grocery stores and clothing shops and barber shops and hair salons and car repair shops.

He had developed an uncanny sense of timing which enabled him to magically appear at construction sites during lunch or coffee breaks. During the winter months he managed to endear himself to the ski patrolmen on Aspen Mountain, and during the summer months (which we spent on Cape Cod) Cajun quickly became an infamous wedding crasher (well over 100 weddings), and participated in numerous other celebrations from birthday parties to baby showers to Bar Mitzvahs.

All of which is by way of explaining that, as mentally fragile as he was, and as intense as his abandonment issues were, Cajun concluded that it was not at all unreasonable for him to wander when and where he wanted, invited or not. He was, in short, a peculiar mix of: neurotic, independent, charming, determined, fragile, vulnerable, adventurous, completely engaging and sweet.

Always, the very best dog he could be.

CHAPTER FIVE

Lost Man, Lost Dog

A few weeks after bringing Cajun home from the shelter, Mark and I decided to take all three dogs on a hike about fifteen miles east of Aspen near the Continental Divide. Autumn in the Rockies is magnificent, even though it's short-lived, beginning in late September and oftentimes ending only a few weeks later when the snow flies. On this first hike with Cajun the leaves were turning color, the air was crisp and dry, and the sky was crystal blue.

Aspen is surrounded by the White River National Forest, named after the White River which runs through the northern section of Colorado. It comprises 2,285,970 acres or 3,571 square miles, is home to ten peaks that are Fourteeners (peaks that have an elevation higher than 14,000 feet), and is an abundant habitat for elk, moose, deer, mountain sheep, mountain goats, mountain lions, bears, bobcats, lynx, marmots, eagles, red-tailed hawks, and thousands of other wildlife species.

Many of the north-facing slopes are blanketed by Douglas fir and blue spruce trees, the needles of which are so deep, dark green as to appear blue. Thick colonies of aspen trees swath the mountainsides, while some of the aspens are scattered among the spruce. During the peak days of autumn, the aspen leaves change from green to orange and gold, and the scrub oak underbrush turns burnt orange, red and brown. And above all of this tower the snow-capped mountain peaks.

While almost any hike in the mountains at this time of year is incredible, this particular hike is truly magnificent, and is called the Lost Man Loop. The trail begins at about 11,505 feet, rises to almost 13,000 feet, and finally ends at 10,520 feet. It is nine miles long, takes about six hours to complete, and requires two cars since it is not a true loop (the loop's beginning and end are separated by about five miles).

The trail starts above timberline, winds through glacierformed tundra and rocks, and passes by Lost Man Lake at 12,815 feet. Tundra wildflowers—marsh marigolds, Parry's clover, king's crown, and alpine phlox—dot the landscape in an array of colors, appearing like a Seurat or Van Gogh pointillist painting. While the trail is not difficult to hike, what might be easy for a person or an average-sized dog to tackle is next to impossible for a miniature dachshund; we quickly ended up carrying Lucy by turn.

Fortunately Rousseau, who weighed about 150 pounds, had no need to be carried. And then there was Cajun, who seemed thrilled about every facet of the outing, from climbing over boulders to wading through swampy marsh grass. There were new smells, new sounds, and new sights for him to behold.

Everything was a curiosity, and within the first few hundred yards of the trail Cajun came upon a couple well camouflaged white-tailed ptarmigan, which suddenly appeared a short distance away in the scrub brush of the tundra. After being mesmerized by them and trying to decide whether or not to try to chase them down, the ptarmigan disappeared as quickly as they had appeared.

Soon other creatures appeared that he had never before seen—there were a number of small brown pikas standing on different rocks and yipping and barking with their high pitched voices, and above them we saw a few mountain goats easily negotiating the cliffs. Cajun's introduction to mountain wildlife was clearly exciting for him, but also seemed to be a bit overwhelming, as he uncharacteristically stayed by our side for the first hour of our hike.

A couple of miles along the trail we arrived at the Lost Man Lake, where the dogs lapped up the clear, cold water as we watched a couple of hikers navigate the imaginary line called the Continental Divide—a divide that separates the watersheds that will either flow westward and drain into the Pacific Ocean, or flow eastward and drain into the Atlantic Ocean, Gulf of Mexico, or the Caribbean Sea. At an elevation of 12,000 feet, a person is gazing at a stretch of the Rockies that can't help but bring out a profoundly humbling sense of the magnificence of it all. While the dogs obviously wouldn't intellectualize about these things, I am fairly certain they have their own instinctive appreciation for these mountains. After taking a water break, we continued along the trail, which soon began its descent from the rocks and tundra into a thick forest of spruce and aspen trees that runs alongside a marsh and Lost Man Creek. It was about ten o'clock in the morning by then, and we had just begun to feel the glare and heat from the sun; entering into the shade of the forest was a relief for both us and for the dogs.

Once we were within this less exposed part of the trail, Cajun seemed more comfortable, and he began to wander a short distance off the path in order to take in the new scents. His nose twitched as he most likely picked up the smell of coyote, elk, bear, mountain lion, or fox, and his ears, which usually lay flat against his head, were now slightly raised. We kept an eye out as he began to explore.

While we mused about these things and watched as Cajun sniffed, marked trees, and explored his new surroundings, something suddenly caught his attention. He looked up and stared across the river... and then he bolted. He took off through the thick willows beside the marsh and dashed across the river... and then he disappeared. We couldn't see him anywhere!

I kept thinking that at any second I would see his yellow coat appear amidst the brush, but I didn't and Mark didn't. We called for him. We shouted and yelled and whistled. But he still didn't appear.

We looked to Rousseau and Lucy for a hint as to his whereabouts, but they weren't lending any clues. Dogs have keen social cognition, and they can and do quickly interpret social cues given by one another. Did they know he was going to bolt? Did they accept it?

Did they care?

While Rousseau and Lucy were not predisposed to roam or run off, they didn't seem at all surprised that Cajun had. Perhaps they instinctually understood that this young male would roam because that is what he did. While they might be curious about the elk and coyote smells, they wouldn't have taken off trying to hunt them down.

But whether or not the two had an instinct about any or all of this, it would later become apparent that Rousseau never approved of Cajun's disappearing acts. When he wandered off, she became agitated and wouldn't settle down until he returned. When he did finally come back she would tower over him and gently take the scruff of his neck between her teeth as an admonishment, making it clear that she was not pleased by his shenanigans.

However, on this occasion, what was supposed to have been a fine and glorious autumn hike turned into a grueling search, as we proceeded to spend the next six hours looking for Cajun. We had begun this adventure at 6:00 a.m., figuring that way we would be done by 1:00 p.m. at the latest. But now it was mid-morning, and we were nowhere near the end of the hike; instead, we were at the beginning of a long and exhausting search for Cajun.

Mark and I spent two hours calling, whistling, and wandering through the brush and between the trees, navigating the marsh and hopping across rocks to cross the river, but we saw no sign of our dog. Finally we decided to split up, hike different trails, and meet up at the Lost Man Reservoir which was very close to the end of the Loop where one of our cars was parked.

Mark took off in one direction by himself, and I in another with Rousseau and Lucy. When it became apparent that my crew was exhausted and had no desire to participate in searching for the newcomer, I decided to head down early to the Reservoir where they could swim and wade in the water while we waited for Mark... who would hopefully soon return with Cajun.

At the Reservoir a few groups of fishermen were casting for trout, while other people could be seen setting out on or returning from day hikes, and still others were just sitting by the water reading or snoozing. I asked almost every one of them if they had seen a yellow dog that looked like a lab wandering around.

"Yellow dog?" one fisherman asked.

"Yes... sort of looks like a lab."

"What's his name?"

"Cajun?" I told him.

"Cajun? Huh. Southern dog?"

"Well yes, sort of. Used to be."

"Used to be southern?"

"Yes."

"There is no such thing. Once southern... always southern," the obviously southern fisherman said, smiling.

"Guess so. Have you seen him?"

"Nope. Been here two hours and never seen a yellow dog pass by."

"Thanks. If you see him and I'm not around, I would really appreciate it if you could bring him back to town and give me a ring. My number is on his collar," I told him.

"What if he isn't wearing a collar?"

I gave the man my name and number, just in case.

"No problem. Will do. Southern yellow dog named Cajun. Got it."

"Thanks. Appreciate it."

About an hour later Mark appeared—but without Cajun. He had hiked for miles. He was exhausted and worried, but not about to give in. Once he knew I hadn't seen him either, he again headed out.

Two hours later there was still no Cajun, and with Mark out searching I broke down in tears, considering the hundred-and-one possibilities that could have happened to our dog in the wilderness.

Guilt-ridden, I berated myself for having taken him on the hike in the first place, for not keeping him leashed, for being a bad foster parent, for being so irresponsible, for absolutely everything and anything.

I kept looking from one mountainside to the other, hoping I would catch a glimpse of him. After a while I realized that Lucy, Rousseau and I were the only ones left at the reservoir; the fishermen had packed up their gear and left, and the hikers who had come to spend the day were all gone.

A mountain autumn chill had settled in, and I'd brought only a light jacket, Mark only a sweatshirt. Dusk was approaching and the sun would soon disappear over the peaks to the west. We had been fortunate that no storms had rolled in that afternoon, but soon it would be dark and quite cold.

Pikas were chirping on the boulders across the reservoir, demanding that we leave the area since it was rightly their home.

Marmots were popping their heads out every once in awhile to see if we had yet departed and it was safe to move about without being bothered by strangers.

As the valley quieted and grew darker, the elk would begin to descend into the area to graze and quench their thirst. I began to worry that Mark might continue his search into the night. I rarely worry about being in the wilderness— while hiking I have come across bears and mountain lions, coyote and fox, but they usually have their own agenda and are not interested in humans unless threatened—but now I began to worry about everything.

While fretting over all these possibilities, I suddenly sensed that something or someone was behind me and quickly spun around... there, trotting along the trail, with his tail wagging and that stupid dog smile on his face was Cajun!

He seemed excited, though not necessarily surprised, to see us... as if we were supposed to be waiting for him.

I jumped up and yelled "Cajun! Cajun! Come." And he came running now towards Rousseau, Lucy, and me, tail swishing as if everything was fine and nothing had happened out of the ordinary. What could possibly be wrong?

"Cajun, what the hell!" I grumbled as he came up beside me and happily tossed his head. "Where

were you?" I questioned, but of course he wouldn't tell me. Rousseau stood over Cajun trying to take his neck in her mouth, and Lucy, who was most often non-judgmental about these things, was simply happy to see Cajun and wagged her own tail in approval.

"Damn. You're here but now we have to find Mark." And then in the distance I could see Mark heading our way.

"Cajun's here," I called out.

Mark called back, "What? Damn... son of a bitch!"

CHAPTER SIX

Cajun and the Cops

I have an aversion to animals being caged, chained, tied down, cooped up, or leashed without very compelling reasons. While I understand the necessity of crating or leashing, on some occasions, it still goes against my inclinations to confine animals. I am the person who opens windows to let flies out, carefully guards spiderwebs from destruction, saves worms from drowning in puddles during rainstorms, and whenever possible avoids stepping on ants. I hate to see parakeets, canaries, and cockatiels in bird cages, turtles or snakes in terrariums, gerbils and hamsters in enclosures, and fish swimming circles in aquariums. As for the "animal business"—little of it works for me: simply driving by a feedlot makes me cringe. So it comes as no surprise that I don't like to leash my dogs unless I am in circumstances that require it for their safety, or the safety of people or wildlife. Fortunately, I live in a semi-rural area and take my dogs hiking in unpopulated areas where they can often, though not always, walk and run off-leash.

That being said, it required a complete adjustment and re-evaluation of my beliefs when Cajun came into my life. I have never really had a dog that roamed... most enjoyed staying by my side and being wherever I was.

As it turned out, Cajun would require of me a change of mind, if not a complete about-face with my thinking on the subject. Initially, the way I dealt with Cajun's roaming was that I didn't deal with it. I opened the door, I let him out, I allowed him his freedom, and then I spent an inordinate number of frustrating hours searching for him.

The entire charade was absurd and I knew it, but locking him in or chaining him up was equally difficult for me. I dithered for awhile before I decided to install an invisible fencing system, since regular fences in mountainside snow country, where five or six or fifteen feet of snow might well accumulate during any winter, is often impractical.

I located a company that put electric fences around properties, and within days a very nice gentleman came out to give me an estimate on installing the fencing and training our dog. I told him about Cajun, and he mentioned that there are some dogs that are hell bent on taking off no matter what you put up, and those dogs are most likely going to run through an electrical fence and take the jolt for their freedom.

So rather than spend a few thousand dollars on fencing that might or might not work, I decided that I would keep Cajun inside more; but, when not inside, I would hike him so many miles and for so many hours that he wouldn't have the energy or the desire to take off. So, over the next two months I undertook this mission. I ran with him every morning, at mid-day I walked him a couple of miles, and then later in the afternoon I took him out again for a long walk.

Lucy and Rousseau joined us only for the mid-day and later walks but not the morning runs. The regimen was ridiculous and time consuming, and I was beyond exhausted!

As for Cajun? He loved it. After all, he was young, full of energy, and excited to be out discovering new smells and places.

Ultimately, my plan to exhaust him so that he wouldn't wander off was a complete failure. The more he roamed, the more he wanted to roam—although soon, instead of wandering the mountains and valleys, Cajun decided to pay a visit to the Aspen Police Department.

It was late October. An autumn snowstorm had blown in over the southwestern peaks and blanketed the town, so Mark and I decided to take a walk on a trail alongside the river that runs through the valley. It was a cold morning, and large wet snowflakes fell from low hanging clouds. This was Cajun's first experience with snow, as far as we knew, and he seemed particularly edgy, so we decided to keep him on the leash.

The snow was beginning to collect on the branches of the blue spruce trees, and crystals of ice were beginning to form in eddies and around river rocks. Cajun was excited by the snow and the crisp air, so when he tried to roll in a snow-bank and became entangled with the leash, I unhooked the clasp and let him go free. He seemed content to stick close by. Mark threw a few snowballs for him to catch, but we soon discovered that among the many things that Cajun did not do was catching or retrieving—anything. We shrugged and continued walking along the riverbank, and the experience felt very peaceful... until all of a sudden three loud gunshots resounded!

It was hunting season, and though we weren't in an area where hunters would or should have been shooting, any loud noise that is set off in the mountains will echo from one mountainside to another.

Hearing the shots Cajun's ears perked up, his eyes widened, and then he bolted. Clearly petrified by the noise, he took off and ran through the snow, and when he came to the riverbank he didn't hesitate—he dashed into the river and swam across to the other side. We called out, but being in a panic he wasn't capable of listening. We watched as he disappeared into a thick grove of aspen trees.

More shots resounded and I knew Cajun was probably running faster than he had before, trying to get away from the nameless fear chasing him. He was less going somewhere than simply getting away from one place in particular—here. After weaving through the trees and following an animal trail that ran along the foothills, we realized that catching up to Cajun was unlikely; we returned to the car, thinking that we might spot him as we drove down the road.

We spent the next four hours looking for him, but to no avail, so we returned home hoping that someone might have left a message telling us that they'd found him. Cajun was wearing his new collar with two different phone numbers attached, and just as we pulled into the driveway my cell phone rang— it was the Aspen Police Department.

Cajun, they told me, was hanging out down at the station.

The members of the Aspen Police Department are local men and women who tend to be down-to-earth, helpful, and friendly. When Mark and I arrived at the station it was very quiet. It was Sunday, the "off season", when there tends to be a low key atmosphere to the town, which is true for the police department too. The crime rate is not high in Aspen anytime, but during the high ski or summer seasons there are more bar fights, street fights, disturbances, break-ins, thefts, and drunk driving arrests than during the off season.

Apparently Cajun had decided to take advantage of the off-season low-key atmosphere, and two policemen had taken on the task of attending to their new guest. We were informed that no paperwork was necessary, no jail time either. Cajun had endeared himself by walking into the station, engaging with whomever was there, and now was sprawled out on the floor having his belly rubbed by one officer, while another offered him treats and water.

"Cajun, look who's come to get you," one of the officers said.

Cajun looked up at us, then rolled onto his back for more attention. "Nice set up you have here, Cajun," I remarked.

"Friendly guy. Not big on treats, but loves the attention," the officer told us.

"No kidding. We are so sorry about this... he's a Katrina rescue, got freaked by the sound of a gunshot and took off. Really sorry," Mark replied.

"No problem. He's good company, but probably best to keep an eye on him during hunting season. He clearly likes to go his own way," the officer responded.

"That's a fact."

It took a bit of coaxing but finally Cajun agreed to come home and honor us with his company.

CHAPTER SEVEN

Top of the Mountain:
The Aspen Ski Patrol Meets Cajun

In the middle of February 2007, when Cajun had been a member of our family for two and a half years, the central Rocky Mountains was slammed with an epic snowstorm. The snow was calculated in feet, not inches. The roads had already been snow packed, but now walls of snow edged either side. The mountains measured over ten feet of snow, plus new powder on top, and our roof was piled four or five feet high; the hotels were busy, the restaurants, bars, and nightclubs were filled nightly, and the town was enjoying a terrific winter season.

Winter in the Rockies, no matter how much it snows or how cold it gets, is not like winter in the northeast. It is not humid—the air in the Rockies is dry and crisp, the sky frequently bright blue with only a few puffy white clouds over the peaks. While the thermometer might read five degrees, people can be stripping off parkas, hats, and gloves because they feel too hot. It is easy to spend the entire day outdoors downhill skiing, snowshoeing, cross-country skiing, or hiking without feeling frigid or uncomfortable no matter the temperature.

Cajun had a thick, multi-layered coat, which meant that he had no problem whatsoever being outside in sub-zero temperatures. In fact, he enjoyed it. So, I wasn't really shocked or surprised when I received a telephone call at 6:30 a.m. from a nice man who worked at the Molly Gibson Lodge in the heart of town, telling me, "Your yellow dog is in our swimming pool."

I had let Cajun out an hour or so earlier, and he had taken a walk into town—a little over a mile away—as he sniffed each peed-on bush and tree. I would assume, having checked out more than a few back alley dumpsters, when he came to the Molly Gibson Lodge he might have been thirsty... and seeing a pool filled with water he probably decided to dip his tongue in for a drink, and then one thing probably led to another, and there he was swimming in the pool.

I doubted Cajun had taken off that morning intending on taking a swim, since he never was much of a swimmer; don't get me wrong, he *would* swim— but he preferred not to.

"Oh. I'm so sorry." I said. "I'll be right down."

45

I threw on my parka, hopped in my truck and drove into town to the lodge. As soon as I arrived, I checked out the pool area and didn't see any sign of Cajun, so I went to the front desk to see if the manager knew where he might have gone. The manager told me that shortly after he called, Cajun climbed out of the pool and ran off.

"Did you see which way he went?" I asked.

"It looked like he was heading toward the mountain," the manager replied, nodding his head south toward Aspen Mountain, just five blocks from the Molly Gibson Lodge.

I thanked him and took off in my truck to search, driving towards the base of the mountain but seeing no sign of Cajun. I drove the streets of the downtown area and still caught no glimpse of him; I circled around the residential areas and saw quite a few other dogs, but no Cajun. After an hour I headed back home, hoping once again for that telephone call that would tell me where my dog might have wandered.

When I got home there were no messages on my answering machine, so I decided I should head out again and search. However, just as I was walking out the front door my telephone rang. I answered and the man on the other end of the line said, with an Australian accent—Aspen is home to quite a number of Aussie transplants—and in a very chipper voice, "Top of the mountain here. Sunny and about ten degrees up top... getting ready for a terrific morning..."

As he continued on in his cheery voice I tried to figure out what was going on. He then said, "Thirty or more new inches of fresh powder and we're getting ready for a wonderful day... and, oh, by the way... Cajun has joined us up top of the mountain for morning donuts and coffee."

"Up top? You mean—the top of the mountain?" I questioned, truly shocked this time.

"I sure do. He came up just a little bit ago, panting pretty heavily after his hike to the top, so we offered him a bowl of water, which he lapped right up, and then he thanked us with a tail wag. Great dog, and as much as we all enjoy his company, the mountain is about to open for the powder hounds (skiers) and from the looks of it he didn't pay for a season pass, and he doesn't have any ski gear," the ski patrolman told me.

"Oh man. I can't believe it. I'm so sorry... and thank you. I'll come up right away... I'm so sorry."

I was sorry.

"No problem. He is a terrific guest. We'll just put him on the gondola and send him down. You can pick him up at the bottom. Have a great day now," the patrolman said before he hung up the phone.

"Oh my God," I said to no one. "Damn! They are going to put Cajun on the gondola? Uh-oh." The gondola ride from top to bottom only takes about fourteen minutes, and as I quickly headed back into town I was considering all the ways that this could end up being one hell of a costly ride.

I could only imagine what Cajun might do while alone in that cable car as it began to make its descent down the mountain—about a 3,000 foot drop—swaying back and forth, rumbling along the cable that hung hundreds of feet above the ground. Would Cajun look out the gondola window and panic? Did dogs experience either acrophobia or vertigo? Would he start chewing on the gondola seats? Would he scratch the windows and the seat material? And just how much would it cost to replace the interior of a gondola car?

In my rush, I parked illegally on Durant Street which runs alongside the base of Aspen Mountain, and ran up the stairs leading to the plaza where the gondola arrives and departs to take skiers to the top of the mountain. Since it was a beautiful day, and there was epic fresh powder from the previous night's snowfall, there was a fairly long line of skiers waiting for the mountain to open so that they could be the first to experience the virgin snow.

I dashed past the skiers, who weren't particularly miffed by my rushing to the head of the line since I wasn't wearing ski clothes or carrying skis, and ran toward the lift operator who was doing his pre-morning check of the gondola cable cars.

"I was told to come down here by the ski patrol because there is a dog that... well... uh .. " I began, and the operator laughed and said with his Australian accent (another Aussie), "Oh right, mate, the yellow pup that's ridin' down for free. That your dog?"

"Yes... he's mine. So sorry about this."

"No problem. From what I've been told, he's a friendly one and likes his morning donuts." He laughed.

"He is friendly. I'm so sorry... But... is he alone?" I asked, fearing the answer.

"Alone, mate?"

"Yes. I mean is he riding the gondola alone?"

"Believe so. Is that a problem?"

"Man... I sure hope not," I sighed, looking up the mountain toward the cars that were coming down, one by one.

Before the gondola cars arrive into the plaza area—about two hundred yards up the mountain—there is a steep descent and an operator (or a dog owner) standing at the plaza watching the cars come in can easily see who, if anyone (or dog), is in the arriving car. Both the lift operator and I were watching each car as it descended the mountain, keeping our eyes out for a dog (in particular, yes, my dog) to be in one of those cars.

The lift operator was excited to have something different and new going on this morning, and I was anxiously considering how much that gondola interior was going to cost me. Five thousand? Two thousand? Ten? How much could a cable car cost?

Many of the waiting skiers were also watching as the cars descended, since word had gotten out that before the mountain opened there would be a gondola bringing down a dog that had been at the top of the mountain enjoying donuts.

Luckily for us, Aspen is a dog-friendly town—a lot of people love and have dogs as companions, and dogs are routinely invited into stores—so the skiers were not upset about having to wait.

Finally, a couple hundred feet up the mountain, I could see the cable car carrying a yellow dog—*my* yellow dog, of course. There was Cajun, sitting in the forward seat, with those big brown eyes and floppy yellow ears, nose to the window, staring straight down the mountain; and, he was completely enjoying the ride!

As one person after another in the ski line also noticed him staring out the window, shouts went up:

"Hey there, yellow dude riding down the mountain! Snow dog on the down. Hey there dude-dog, how were the freshies?"

Then they all started cheering as the car carrying Cajun came closer to the plaza. I was happy they were all happy, but I was still worried about the inside of that car: how bad was it?

The car swung into the plaza and the lift operator stopped the gondola, opened the door, and Cajun jumped out, like he'd been doing it all his life. I quickly peeked inside the cabin, and thankfully saw no rips, tears, or scratches! Cajun had been a gentleman rider on the way down.

"Cajun... good boy," I said, as he spun in a circle and smiled at me. The line of skiers roared. Cajun turned to his crowd, wagged his tail, and took another spin for their entertainment.

"Yeah dude. You go boy. How was it up there? Good going? Powder deep above your head? Nice. Sweet. Awesome," the line of skiers shouted to Cajun.

My eyes welled with tears, since it was just so damn nice that this dog, who lived on the streets of New Orleans in such sorry circumstances, who had gone through the horrors and trauma of Hurricane

Katrina, who would have died from heartworm were it not for being rescued, who had been taken from all he knew to this strange environment, was now being so warmly welcomed—and he was so obviously happy to be here.

I leashed Cajun, thanked the lift operator profusely, walked by the line of skiers and thanked them, too, for their kindness.

Cajun wagged his thanks.

CHAPTER EIGHT

Born Rider:
The Uninvited Guest

As Rousseau, Lucy, Cajun, and I fine-tuned our lives together, we became bonded. In some respects they reacted to me in much the same way my children react to me: I would carry on conversations and they would pretend to listen. I would ask their opinion and they rarely offered it. I would diligently and faithfully cook meals for them and clean up after them, and they would never thank me. I would turn down the heat, turn off the lights, and close the front door after they waltzed in leaving it ajar, do the grocery shopping, and pay the bills with far too little appreciation for what was being done.

Certainly there were times that the kids thanked me and the dogs wagged their tails, but less often than probably should have happened. It surely began to seem to me that the dogs had fallen into similar patterns as my children, because I spoil them all equally. There were some obvious differences—for example, the dogs didn't come home at three in the morning, they didn't bring home new girlfriends (some of whom I liked and others who made me more than a bit nervous), they didn't go to colleges or graduate schools that required burdensome tuition payments. The dogs were also not known to leave their parkas on the banister, misplace their shoes, keys, and sunglasses, or drop their iPods or cell phones in the toilet.

However, the dogs, unlike my children, were unapologetic about tracking snow and mud into the house, were pleased and proud to deliver their dug-up dog bones as gifts, were nonchalant about drooling while drinking water, and unhesitatingly passed gas anytime they felt like it; they never gave a thought to offering their help in shoveling snow, stacking firewood, cleaning the driveway, or washing the car. And while I recognize that the dogs are not my children and my children are not my dogs, I must confess that the lines sometimes became blurred.

The bottom line was that the dogs and I became our own little family. And typical of many families, we created and then followed our own pleasant routine which veered only by virtue of necessity— which could mean anything from health concerns to thunderstorms.

As the dogs aged, health became a major factor in reconfiguring what took place from one day to the next. For example, when it became clear that both Rousseau and Lucy couldn't handle long hikes or walks over a mile anymore because of Rousseau's ongoing joint problems (fairly typical of large dogs) and Lucy's age (she was 17) and size, we had to accommodate and adjust.

It was not simply that I was trying to do my best for both Rousseau and Lucy; it was also because they no longer wanted to go on the long morning hikes, which they made clear by not even trying to get up when I went to the front door. They let me know what they wanted and I understood.

Hence we began a new morning routine, one where I took off with just Cajun, while Rousseau and Lucy seemed quite content to stay at home and sleep or discuss dog issues with one another. When Cajun and I would return a few hours later, I always heaped attention on the other dogs, since I believe that dogs have an acute sense of fairness. They are very much like children in that way too—and I strove to give them each an equal amount of my time and attention.

So each morning after Rousseau and Lucy had been outside for a short walk, Cajun and I would take on a much longer hike. During the winter months we would begin a few miles away on Independence Pass. From November through May, the road leading over Independence Pass is closed since it is not uncommon for over twenty feet of snow to fall up there; given the high avalanche probability, it would be impossible in such a case to keep the road clear.

Once the gate at the bottom of the Pass is swung shut and locked, the only traffic you'll find on the road is people walking, snowshoeing, skiing, bicycling, or riding a snowmobile or snow cat. It is a quiet and beautiful place to hike, and when Cajun and I would arrive almost every winter morning just after sunrise, we would be the only ones there. Most people wait for the sun to rise higher in the sky and warm the mountain air before setting out, but Cajun—who was easily intimidated by other dogs—preferred the solitude of the early morning.

There was one exception, however. During busy holiday ski weekends, it would not be uncommon for us to run into more people, other dogs, and a few local skiers riding snowmobiles into the back country looking to ski the deep powder. And sometimes, during those weeks, professional snowmobile operators guide groups up the Pass for special events, snow picnics, and other outings. Cajun had shown little interest when these snowmobile groups passed by, but I would soon find out that was not always the case.

As things seemed to go with the adventures of Cajun, on one particular occasion he decided he would join in on a snowmobile trip. It was President's Day weekend, and the town was especially busy. The town was crowded with people enjoying the mountains, the fresh snow, skiing, and snowmobiling. I hadn't really given much thought to it being a holiday, so Cajun and I went out for our morning hike, as usual. It was a crystal clear morning—blue skies and just a slight breeze—so we hiked quite a ways up Independence Pass before turning around and heading back down.

As we descended the mountain I heard the buzz of snowmobiles coming toward us, and within minutes twelve of them raced around a curve in the road. It was a snowmobile party; there was a guide in the lead, and as soon as he spotted Cajun and me hiking down the road he politely motioned for the others to slow. Behind the guide, now at a much reduced pace, were ten snowmobiles, some with kids riding on the seat behind, everyone bundled in for the weather in warm clothes, ski masks, and goggles.

Bringing up the rear was a second guide, who pulled an attached sled packed with food and drinks. I don't know what piqued Cajun's interest as they went by—the number of loud engines, the kids waving and hollering, the sled pulled behind, the smell of food on that sled—but as soon as that last snowmobile went by and they resumed their speed, Cajun took off after them.

"Cajun! Cajun! Cajun..." I shouted—not that he could hear me over the din of the snowmobiles—but he wasn't about to come back even if he had heard. With his typical obsessive determination, his single-minded focus was only on catching up to those snowmobiles.

From that point to the top of Independence Pass is about nine miles—nine vertical miles that rise from approximately 8,500 feet to 12,000 feet—and though the snowmobile party wasn't going to the top of the Pass, they were going within two miles and a thousand feet short of it.

If Cajun was going to follow them to where they were going to stop and enjoy a picnic—which he was—then he was about to run seven miles uphill and make an ascent of some 3,000 feet. I stopped shouting Cajun's name as he disappeared around a curve a quarter mile up the road, realizing the futility of it.

"Damn," I said to no one, as I stared at the snowmobile tracks and Cajun's paw prints and tried to decide whether I should follow them up the mountain. That consideration was short-lived, though, since I hadn't brought along water and wasn't prepared to hike seven miles up and then back down again.

I figured that the snowmobile party was not likely to picnic near the top of the Pass for more than a couple of hours before they'd head down again, so my best option was simply to return to the area where all the cars were parked and wait.

It was a sunny day, and by the time I reached the parking lot quite a few people were beginning to arrive to hike the pass. I hung out near the gate and watched as people arrived, strapped on snowshoes or clicked into their crosscountry skis, and took off. While waiting I met a man who told me he had been on one of those snowmobile picnics before.

Him: "Yep. I went on one of those picnics a couple of years ago. Lots of fun."

Me: "Oh really?"

Him: "They took us up to the old ghost town. Ever been up there?"

Me: "Yes, I have."

Him: "That's somethin' up there. They said those cabins were built in 1879 when some gold prospectors hit a vein. Imagine that huh? Living up there through those winters... had to have been a tough life... don't you think?"

Me: "Yes, it must have been."

Him: "Those prospectors though... tough people... they made half a million bucks mining that vein. And they managed to find a way to live in those cabins through one storm after another for eleven years before they finally had to give up after being hit by a particularly wicked storm. Did you hear about that?"

Me: "Yes, that's right." I was surprised he knew so much of the history of the Independence Ghost Town.

Him: "That's what the guides told us."

Me: "Sounds like it was a good time."

Him: "And the food they brought up was damn good."

Me: "Is that right?"

Him: "We had fun up there. Are you a local?"

Me: "Yes."

Him: "Lived here long?"

Me: "Forty-some years."

Him: "That *is* local. Are you waiting on someone?"

Me: "Sort of... I took a hike this morning and my dog chased after the snowmobiles as they were on their way up. I'm just waiting for them to come back down... hopefully he'll follow them down too."

Him: "Is that right? That's one heck of a run up."

Me: "He is one heck of a stubborn dog."

Him: "They'll bring him back down. Nice folks those guides. Real nice."

Me: "I'm definitely glad to hear that."

Him: "Could be a while though. Four hours... maybe... give or take."

Me: "Four hours?" Ugh.

Him: "Yep. Just about."

Me: "Four hours. Dang."

Him: "Long wait for a dog."

Me: "Yes. Yes it is."

So for the next few hours I both patiently and impatiently waited. I ran into some friends who were setting out on a nice hike with their well-behaved dogs. I watched people come and go. I watched an eagle circle above and then land on an overhanging high cliff. I listened to some noisy crows argue. I wondered if Cajun was having a nice lunch with his new friends since I was fairly certain he had ingratiated himself with his typical Cajun charm.

It was a long wait, but no matter how impatient I grew, there was no choice but to wait for the group to come back down and hope Cajun was with them.

About three hours in, I heard in the distance the distinct whine of snowmobile engines. Anxious to know whether Cajun was with the group, I began to hike back up the trail. And finally, the snowmobiles—in a line, one after the next— came round the bend in the road. Sure enough, in the front seat of that lead snowmobile, being held tightly by the rider, yellow ears flapping in the wind, grinning cheek to cheek, was none other than my ever-so-loyal companion, Cajun. He couldn't have been more pleased with himself, riding in the front seat of the contraption with his new buddy, feeling the wind on his face and nice strong arms gripping his belly.

As Cajun's new friends journeyed closer to where I was standing, I waved my arms to signal the guide to stop. Cajun looked over at me nonchalantly: he was not in the least bit ashamed or guilty about his disappearance—he'd had a good run, met some terrific people, eaten a delicious lunch, and managed to catch a ride down the mountain—what was there to feel guilty about?

Why hadn't I come along?

Where had I been all this terrific time?

The guide stopped his machine, smiled and nodded at me, and then turned to Cajun and said: "So, hey friend, nice meeting up with you. I think this is where you get off buddy. Thanks for joining us, dude. Next time."

Cajun jumped off, shook his head happily, spun in a few circles, and then ran up to me, tail wagging.

"Was that fun Cajun? Nice day?" I asked.

"He did seem to have a nice day," the guide smiled.

"I'm really sorry he followed you," I said ruefully, smiling back.

Why was I always stuck apologizing for Cajun's actions?

"No worries. We loved him. Poor guy was thirsty by the time he reached the top, so we gave him some water. And after he finished that off he joined us for some buffalo wings for lunch. All the kids loved having him along... he's a great party dog."

"Yeah, he does like a good party." I agreed.

"He really does. And then I thought he might like to try riding lead back down the mountain. He seemed to like that too. Born rider, isn't he?"

"Seems that way." I nodded.

I thanked the guide again and put Cajun on a leash. "Buffalo wings, huh? Don't get used to that."

CHAPTER NINE

2,272 Miles:

Driving Cross Country with Three Dogs

When people ask me why we drive 2,272 miles from Aspen, Colorado to Truro, Massachusetts every June—and then return again from Truro to Aspen in August—I have two responses: "how else" and "why not".

How else: Why don't I fly with three dogs from Aspen to Denver, Denver to Boston, and finally Boston to Provincetown? Then turn around and repeat that particular adventure at the end of the summer?

Well, for two reasons: 1. I used to do that many years ago, but the airlines have changed their rules and no longer allow one passenger to take more than one dog on a flight. This means I would have to pay for two other people to join me in order to get three dogs on board. 2. Flying is dangerous for the dogs for a host of reasons—temperature extremes (both hot and cold), they can get put on the wrong planes (it happened to me once when my Golden Retriever, Tennessee was put on a plane to Milwaukee, Wisconsin instead of Boston, Massachusetts), it's hard on dogs physically and mentally, and it's expensive to fly three dogs and three people round trip. A trip from Aspen to Denver to Boston to Provincetown for three dogs and three people would be more than I would care to calculate.

So driving it is.

All of which is by way of explaining that driving long distances with dogs is not really a choice; it's not something most people would choose to do, unless they love to drive and own a large RV, were able to be medicated 24/7 while someone else drove, or were running from the law.

Driving over 2,000 miles with three dogs requires grit, tenacity, lots of strong coffee, a large car or truck, and open windows.

Once, about ten years ago, I made the foolish mistake of trading in my roomy Chevy Suburban for a BMW Sport Station Wagon. I have no idea what I was thinking, save for the fact that I had been driving Suburbans in order to haul my kids to either hockey games or tennis matches or equestrian events for many years; so when my youngest child graduated from high school and went off to college, I thought it would be nice to have a smaller, spiffy sort of ride that might be fun to drive.

The BMW *was* fun to drive, but when June rolled around and it was time for Mark and me to load the car up for the trip across the country, it took me only five minutes to realize that I had made a very, very bad choice. Two months later I traded that nice, speedy little wagon in for what is called a "couch car"—which is really a truck that has been fine tuned for families and people who need to haul things (or dogs) from place to place—a large GMC Yukon.

Granted, the Yukon was harder to park in tight spaces and it guzzled gasoline, and it most certainly takes longer to wash and detail a Yukon, but I wouldn't trade my truck in for a smaller car unless I went down to only one dog, which is unlikely.

The drive cross country is a two-person/three-dog operation. Mark and I take this trek as seriously as people preparing for ironman triathlons. We plan it, we gear up for it, and we attack it.

Even though this is ideally a two man/woman operation, there have been occasions in which each of us has taken the trip solo—something I would never recommend. It is challenging in every conceivable way, from walking three dogs at rest stops, to checking into motels, to going to the restroom when it's simply too hot to leave the dogs in the car with rolled up windows.

After years of dog-tripping, Mark and I have developed a working formula to make the trip go as smoothly as possible. It is not an art form, nor is it a business; it is really a personally crafted formula. Much of this crafted formula has grown from trial and error, semi-disaster, mini-disaster, slight problems, and major issues, which is the way most formulas are born.

It is personal because not everyone would chose to travel the way we do. Most people who undertake a 2,272 mile trip do it over a four or five day period, as it takes 36 driving hours door to door. On a good trip—meaning we don't run into heavy rain storms, don't get caught in nightmare traffic jams outside of Chicago or Cleveland or Buffalo, don't get hung up going five miles an hour in more than the usual number of construction zones, don't have any flat tires or automobile breakdowns (the two days spent in Kearney, Nebraska trying to have a transmission rebuilt comes to mind), don't get stopped for speeding tickets (as in going 102 mph in a 75 mph zone), don't lose a dog for extended periods of time, don't miss that very important exit (which has somehow happened three times outside Cleveland, Ohio)—we can get the total drive time down to 35 hours, but that is about as good as it gets.

So, to say the least, spending 35-36 hours of driving with three dogs who inevitably become restless, need a walk, and are farting, scratching, snoring, and spinning in circles, is just not a fun experience. We don't stop off to visit local flea markets (we have our own in the car), we don't take side roads to check out antique stores or museums or places of interest—this is not a fun, entertaining vacation drive.

We load up the car with bags, books, computers, etc., fill up the tank the night before departing, arise at three in the morning and are out the door by 3:30 a.m.

It is now show-time: one person gets behind the wheel, stabs and steers, while the other person tries to nod off and catch some shut-eye. When the tank runs near empty we pull into a gas station, fill up the tank, walk the dogs, water the dogs, feed the dogs, and return to the car, switching driver and passenger positions. We go and go and go. We usually drive 20-21 hours the first day, pulling into a motel wherever we are at midnight or one in the morning.

And this—at midnight or one in the morning— is where the trip has often taken interesting twists. In the early years of these treks, I would make a list of the motels that were pet friendly and either we would make a reservation, or we would simply memorize where they were located.

However, pet-friendly motels are usually (not always) the least desirable and most filthy motels along any highway; since I am a fairly obsessive neat freak, staying at any of these dirt bag motels was a borderline psychotic experience for me. I would enter a room with gloved hands, elbows shoving the door open, never touching anything that I absolutely didn't have to touch. Then I would sleep fully clothed so as not to touch body to bed sheets, and breathe as little as possible during the five or six hours we stayed in one of these places.

Disgusting is a generous word for such motels. Vile would be more accurate. Even my youngest son—an avid outdoorsman who has no problem spending weeks or months at a time trekking the wilderness, not showering, and sleeping in mud-banks if need be—even he balked when at 2:00 a.m. we pulled into a motel in Indiana off I-80.

"Christ, are you serious, Mom?" he asked as walked into the room where spiders crawled up the walls and unidentifiable bugs lounged in the bath-room sink.

"Damn. Don't touch anything. Don't undress, and use your jacket as a pillow," I suggested.

Eventually, when we were told by other pet own-ers that they completely disregarded the motel rules, picked wherever they wanted to stay, and snuck their pets in a back or side door. We were all over that. Quite honestly, I'm not sure why it took Mark and me so long to figure this out, since neither of us is particularly law abiding when it comes to our fam-ily's comfort, but it did.

In any event, once we realized our errant ways, we quickly changed our plan of attack, pulling into newer and cleaner looking motels and sneaking the dogs inside. However, there was a catch for us; most people are sneaking in ONE dog or cat, and usu-ally a smaller one at that, while we needed to sneak THREE dogs into a motel, one of whom weighed about 150 pounds and had the quirky dysfunction of not liking to go up or down strange stairs.

In fact, our girl Rousseau had an outright aversion to it.

Unfortunately, more often than not, most motels have three or four stories, and more often than not (probably because we are one of last to check in for the night) we would be assigned a room on the top floor. It just always happens that way—in much the same way that someone might be so lucky as to win a million dollar lottery more than once (twice is ridiculous)—we are always given a key for a third or fourth floor room.

When pulling into a motel at two in the morning, the driver waits to the side of the building so as not to be seen by the clerk and the passenger checks in and retrieves the inevitable third or fourth floor room key. Then we park near the back of the motel, unload three nervous dogs who badly need to pee, sneak (a ludicrous likelihood) them in the back or side door, coax, carry, plead, and beg them to be quiet as we head up the stairs, hurry down a strange hallway hoping no one exits their room before we find ours, pray for the room key to work, and finally lead three dogs inside a musty room where they collectively rush to the bathroom to be the first head in the toilet for that glorious cold water.

Not surprisingly there are always obstacles.

To begin with, Rousseau (our Newfoundland) always had the stair problem. To be fair to Rousseau, the stair problem was not just limited to stairs—she in fact had an aversion to crossing wooden or metal bridges and overpasses, walking on stone patios, stone walkways, stone decks, marble floors, and any uneven sidewalk.

But stairs, strange stairs in particular, were always the most daunting for her. I have no idea why, since she had been with me since she was eight weeks old, and unless she was dropped down the stairs as a puppy before I knew her, I never saw any reason for the issue to have come about.

In any event, there she would be, unwilling to negotiate the stairs; and when Rousseau set her mind on not doing a thing, there wasn't much hope of changing said mind. Moreover, it is not easy to convince a 150-pound dog to move forward if she (or he) doesn't want to. It would be easier to motivate a stubborn mule to go up those stairs than a determined Newfoundland.

Moreover, standing in the stairwell of a motel which is not pet friendly at one or two in the morning is just not the place or time to start yelling commands at one's unyielding dog. Therefore, the only solution that we were ever able to come up with was to carry Rousseau up the stairs that night, and then back down the stairs the next morning.

Obviously, this is something Mark (or whoever is lucky enough to travel cross country with me) does since I couldn't possibly carry a Newfoundland anywhere without the real likelihood of being hospitalized for months afterwards.

During these late night/early morning events, I would step aside and pray to whatever force might care to listen that Mark wouldn't fall, wrench his back, break a leg, separate a shoulder, or who knows what else.

Rousseau hated being carried, but since she wouldn't budge to negotiate the stairs, she had no choice. Mark would grumble at her and she would obey by leaning into him while being carried like a bride up the stairs.

On a number of occasions we ran into other guests as they were descending or ascending the staircase, and when they saw Mark carrying this giant black dog all sorts of remarks were made: "You have got to be kidding me." "Is that a bear?" "Is it alive?" "Why don't you leave the dog in the car?" "Do you have medical insurance?"

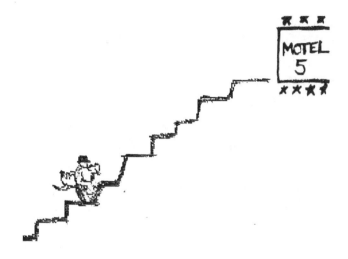

This was, and still is, the main reason we only stay one night in a motel, driving 20-21 hours the first day and 16 the second. One night of carrying any large dog, much less a Newfoundland, up and down multiple flights of stairs is enough.

There have been numerous adventures during these cross country trips. One night Lucy, the mini Dachshund, decided to put a wrench in our motel stay. Lucy loved the motel nights since she was allowed to eat MacDonald's nuggets on the bedspread, and she enjoyed sleeping on the bed with us. However, on this particular occasion, before getting into the room, Lucy had the urge to explore the motel. We had checked in, been given our third floor room assignment as usual, and parked in the back of the motel.

We unloaded the dogs, let them take care of business, and when we slid the key into the back entrance to "sneak in", we realized that in order to get to the stairs we had to open a second door to the stairwell. Before we could open that second door, Lucy took off down the hallway that led directly to the front desk!

Mark ran after her, and I waited with Rousseau and Cajun at the bottom of the stairwell. I watched as Mark dashed down the hall chasing Lucy, but before the dog arrived at the front desk she decided to make the chase even more interesting. Finding herself next to a soda machine, she made a split-second decision and scurried behind the machine into a space that only a miniature Dachshund could possibly fit into.

Lucy was black, small, and clever. Mark is clever but not small. He leaned down and whisper-pleaded with her to come out, "Lucy... come out of there... please. Be a good girl... good dog, Lucy... come on."

Lucy was no fool and wasn't having any part of that. She was perfectly happy exploring behind the soda machine. As Mark knelt on the floor, begging Lucy to come out, the desk clerk appeared from around the corner, asking the obvious, "Lose something sir?"

"Uh... oh no. Thanks though... I was just getting a soda and dropped my quarter," Mark said, now hoping that Lucy stayed where she was and didn't bark.

"Need some help?" the clerk asked.

"Oh, no thanks. I've got it," Mark said, just as Lucy started barking.

"Is that a barking quarter?" the desk clerk smiled at Mark.

"Yeah, it is," Mark said, sheepish now.

"Must be a small barking quarter to fit back there. Good luck with that," the clerk replied and walked away.

Mark could see Lucy staring at him from behind the machine. Frustrated he hissed, "Damn Lucy. Come on out of there." Still nothing. "Fine then... live your friggin' life in Peru, Illinois," he said, then stood up and started walking back down the hallway.

Half way down he could hear Lucy's small feet padding along behind him—he turned around as she trotted unabashedly up to him, putting her front paws on his shins, asking to be carried.

"That was fun, huh Lucy?" He said picking her up.

Next there was the incident with the Nebraska State Patrol. We were on our return trip west from Truro to Aspen. It was the second day of travel and

Mark and I were dogtired, had listened to one or two audio-books, had little left to say to one another, were done with the dogs farting, and were altogether anxious to get home.

We were cruising through Nebraska, which has a speed limit of 75 mph; for most seasoned long distance drivers, this means that you can safely drive 83 mph without getting a ticket. This also happened to have been the year that I owned the BMW sport wagon, pre-trading it in. As such, we'd attached a Yakima carrier on the top of the car—loaded to the brim with luggage—and the interior of the wagon was cramped with the three dogs, Mark, myself, two computers, two night bags, dog dishes, dog blankets, dog food, and a couple of oil paintings that could not be placed in the Yakima.

The car was cargo-heavy, both inside and out. I was driving, putting the pedal to the metal, hoping to get to the Nebraska-Colorado state line so I could happily see the "Welcome to Colorado" sign. We were zipping along I-80 and the speedometer had "somehow" crept up to 102 mph.

I knew that I was clipping along at a high speed, but wanted to get to Julesburg, Colorado by early afternoon, which meant we would be home by early evening. Mark was sleeping, the dogs were snoring, and all was good with the world until I saw in my rear view mirror those infamous flashing red lights coming up behind me.

"Damn!" I said loudly, waking Mark. "I'm busted."

"How fast were you going?" he asked.

"98. Maybe 102." I admitted pulling over to the side of the highway.

"Yeah, you are totally busted," Mark said.

When we came to a stop, I got out my license and insurance information, put down my window, and waited for the Nebraska state trooper to walk up to the door. I watched in my rear view mirror as the trooper remained in his car, running my plates. After a while he slowly opened his car door, got out, and walked up to my window. He was at least six feet tall and overweight by about 75 pounds.

As he leaned over, I could see he had what I can only describe as an unpleasant expression on his face. I didn't say a word, figuring I was screwed and there was no point in trying to argue about my speed. He would happily inform me what he'd clocked me at within seconds.

"License. Proof of insurance," he said, and almost as soon as he finished the word "insurance" Rousseau sat up in the back and barked. She was nowhere near the window but the state trooper, who was obviously shocked by the visual of a very large furry black animal staring at him, over-reacted, straightened up, unsnapped his holster and pulled his gun.

Trooper: "What is that? Make it lie down or I'll shoot it in the head."

Me: "Whoa... she's friendly."

Trooper: "You want to see that—whatever-it-is—dead on the side of the road?"

Me: "No sir."

Trooper: "Put your window down just an inch from the top and pass me the papers. I would sure like to shoot that thing."

Me: "Dog."

Trooper: "What did you say?"

Me: "No problem."

Trooper: "No problem? I'll tell you what is no problem... I would have no problem shooting that thing. Don't mess with me. Got it?"

Me: "Got it."

Mark mumbled: "Asshole."

I mumbled: "Serious asshole."

Trooper: "Did you say something?"

Me: "No sir."

Trooper: "You all want to go to jail? I would be happy to shoot the thing and take you both to jail."

Me: "No sir. Sorry sir. No sir. Sorry."

Mark mumbled: "What a major asshole."

Twenty-five friggin' minutes later, after the cop had taken his merry time trying to remember how to spell, write, and grind his teeth at the same time, he got out of his car, walked back to my window with his hand resting on that gun in the unhitched holster, and motioned for me to put the window down.

Trooper: "Down two inches. Not any more than that."

Me: "Good grief."

Trooper: "What did you say?"

Me: "Nothing."

Trooper: "That thing should be dead."

Then slipped the ticket for one-hundred-twenty-five dollars through the window opening.

"Thank you so very friggin' much," I said as he walked back to his car.

"Asshole. Get the hell out of this damn state," Mark added.

While Nebraska presented challenges, neither Iowa—nor Cajun—were to be left out of our dog incidents during our journeys to and fro. It was the end of August, and we were driving back to Colorado. Midway through Iowa, the dogs were making it clear that they needed to pee, so we pulled over at a rest stop that bordered a corn field.

By this time in the season—late summer—the corn stalks from ground to tassel tip can be quite tall. Most grow ten or fifteen feet, and some even reach twenty or twenty-five feet in height. The rows are carefully planted, going on for acres and acres, a magnificent meeting of nature and man's hand.

We had pulled in at the far end of the rest stop, past the sleeping truckers and a few parked cars, so that the dogs could relieve themselves and we could give them a short walk. When we opened the back door, Cajun bolted from the car, jumping over Rousseau and Lucy in order to get out first. I assumed he needed to pee badly—which may have been the case—but he acted like a dog on a mission; that mission, unfortunately, was to run under the barbed wire fencing that bordered the corn field and disappear amidst the rows of corn stalks.

Me: "Cajun!"

"Cajun, damn it!" Mark shouted as he crawled through the fencing and headed after him.

And down the row he ran. And down the row Cajun ran. Mark repeatedly called for him.

But Cajun was nowhere to be seen as he dodged between stalks and down rows.

Since I was unable to see Cajun, I tried to keep my eye on which row Mark was in, and in which direction he was traveling. I could hear him yelling for Cajun, but that was about the extent of my ability to locate either one of them. After forty-five minutes of running up one row and down another, Mark returned sweating and angry.

"He didn't come back here?" he asked, exhausted. "No. Want me to try?" I asked.

"Damn it. No, I'm going back in," he said, climbing back through the barbed wire.

Another forty-five minutes went by: No Cajun. No Mark. Cajun might have picked up some scent, might have decided he was sick of traveling in the back of the car, or might have decided it was a good time to explore Iowa.

Another thirty minutes later Mark returned, without Cajun.

"What the hell should we do?" he asked. "I can't find him anywhere. There are thousands of acres of corn stalks. How the hell are we supposed to find him in that maze?"

"Should we walk the other dogs up and down the rows and hope they will attract him back?" I suggested.

"I don't think that would work. He's on some damn mission," he fumed.

"God," I said, exasperated.

Three hours later, Cajun showed up smiling and wagging his tail and ready to go home.

CHAPTER TEN

The Wedding Crasher

Even though he was easily intimidated and cautious around other dogs, Cajun was quite notoriously a party animal. Maybe it had something to do with his "upbringing" in New Orleans—where perhaps he mixed it up while wandering through the French Quarter—but whatever the reason, the dog liked a good party. He was always on the lookout to crash a party or any group gathering, and was not discriminating; he saw almost any collection of people as an opportunity to mingle. From construction sites, where he would hang out during coffee or lunch breaks, to formal weddings where he would co-mingle with the guests, Cajun sought out any and all occasions.

He did seem to recognize that attending social events was not like hanging out at a construction site; Cajun clearly found weddings, Bar Mitzvahs, birthday parties, and memorial services more intriguing. This was due in large part, I believe, to the fact that social gatherings were usually catered with excellent food selections, and the people at those events were usually happy, inebriated, and frequently feeling kind-hearted and generous. There were often children there—who he adored—and music, too, which this New Orleans dog definitely enjoyed, another of his unique qualities.

Most dogs do not have the opportunity to be frequent party crashers, but Cajun had multiple opportunities from June through August, as my summer cottage is situated next to a club which is frequently rented out for such events. The Pamet Harbor Yacht and Tennis Club, and probably anyplace that calls itself a "yacht club" for that matter, suggests a Gatsby-like setting, the entrance opening to a winding crushed white gravel driveway, lined by large maple and oak trees. The driveway graciously leads guests to a large English tudor or southern style mansion, with a gabled roof, wraparound porch, and a backdrop of lush gardens surrounding an expensively tiled patio and a large pool.

At the very least, the suggestion exists that this particular club would be a place where people of some wealth would gather to keep their yachts or fine sea-worthy fishing vessels. A "yacht club" implies a venue that is obviously on the waterfront and has at least one pier that can accommodate the members' boating needs.

Suffice it to say that this is not at all what the Pamet Harbor Yacht and Tennis Club actually is. In fact it is the antithesis of that image, save for being on the water. Built over half a century ago, it never was that sort of club to begin with, and Truro has never been known to attract the upper crust who might own yachts or who might be seen dressed in whites for tennis.

Truro, the smallest town on Cape Cod, is built on a narrow strip of land on the outer banks of the Cape Cod peninsula: it is located south and east of the tip of the Cape, is bordered by the towns of

Provincetown to the northwest and Wellfleet to the south,; it is also bordered by the Atlantic Ocean to the north and east, and the Cape Cod Bay to the west. The area was first inhabited by the Wampanoag Native Americans, who called the area Payomet or Pamet, and its European history goes back to 1603 when Captain Martin Pring and his crew anchored along the Pamet River and spent a couple of months exploring the area, meeting the local Natives and learning about their livelihoods.

In 1620 the Mayflower anchored off the Truro shoreline, and sixteen English pilgrims debarked their vessel and explored the Truro area, where they discovered a cache of corn hidden beneath a mound and sighted some Native Americans. They considered staying in the area but ultimately decided otherwise, sailing their ship across the Bay to anchor in what is now called Plymouth.

Some 70 years later (in the 1690's) the town of Truro was settled, and was finally incorporated in 1709. New settlers who inhabited the area made their livelihoods by fishing, whaling, and shipbuilding.

In the late 19th century, the area began to attract a number of writers and artists due to the extraordinary landscape, the unique light, and the acceptance and social openness of the community. By the 20th century, Truro had become known for its arts community, and in 1961 President Kennedy designated sixty-five percent of the land in Truro as part of the Cape Cod National Seashore. This action, while saving the pristine solitude of the area, also ensured it would never see the kind of development that some of the other areas of Cape Cod have witnessed.

All of which is to say that Truro remained off the radar for the well-coiffed set, and the term "yacht club" in Truro does not connote the same meaning as it might in Chatham, Hyannis, Martha's Vineyard, or Nantucket.

The Pamet Yacht and Tennis Club (PHYTC) has two clay courts that are sporadically occupied and moderately well maintained, depending on the club's finances, the rain, and the wind. The "yachting" aspect of the club hardly meets the definition of "yachting", unless that includes spending a day kayaking or canoeing, sailing a sun fish, or fishing from a 22 foot Boston Whaler—there are no yachts. The pier used by the boating members of the club just barely meets what one could describe as a true pier: it is a precarious narrow wooden structure that stretches about twenty yards into the river and is used for tying down dinghies or row boats, not yachts.

Despite the fact that the PHYTC doesn't cater to the upper echelons of yachting, it happens to have one of the most beautiful daytime and evening sunset views anywhere in the world; it overlooks the soft lime green marsh grass that snakes through the Pamet River, and beyond that the Cape Cod Bay. Across the bay is the thin strip of land called Provincetown, with its sparkling night lights.

And since the club is always in need of funds to keep the courts, the old pier, and the run-down clubhouse running and in repair, they finally realized they could capitalize on the view by renting the place out for weddings and other gatherings or party functions. And while the view is incredible, there are a number of factors that keep the rental price down: for example, the clubhouse consists of only one main room, sized at about 20' by 20'; the drinking water has to be brought in by truck since there is no well supplying the yacht club; the bathrooms are small and the sort of bathrooms one would find in an old summer camp for kids; the kitchen is a cramped area with a small refrigerator and stove; there is no real bar, and no fancy chairs or tables or tablecloths.

It is bring your own for everything (from liquor to fineries) and if one wants to host a party for more than 20 guests, a party tent has to be set up in the sand parking lot of the yacht club—which happens frequently.

Which by way of explaining suggests that most folks who rent the PHYTC for a social event are not the type of people who would take offense to seeing a dog wandering about throughout the afternoon or evening. And Cajun was, if nothing else, an opportunist when it came to social events. As soon as he realized that he was welcome at one party, then he quickly assumed that meant he would always be granted an open invitation.

As convenient as it was for Cajun to have parties occurring next door to his home, he didn't feel the need to limit his potential as a wedding crasher. In other words, his wedding wanderings were not solely limited to the PHYTC, as he was infamously known for appearing at quite a few other weddings that occurred in and around Truro.

Between weddings and other events, Cajun had an extremely busy summer social calendar.

It would be impossible to describe all of Cajun's adventures while party crashing, but some are especially noteworthy. Usually we heard the details from the PHYTC manager Charlie, but not infrequently we heard about it from one of the guests. Numerous times we were told stories about Cajun being in the middle of wedding photos—once, in fact, standing between the bride and groom for their photo shoot. Numerous other times we were told that Cajun sat properly and quietly in the front row, watching as the ceremony unfolded. It got to the point that we had requests for Cajun to attend more than one wedding, since his reputation as dog attendee or dog greeter or dog entertainer traveled far and wide.

So, naturally (or not), given these requests and his popularity, we purchased a black bowtie made for dogs that Cajun wore on wedding days. He seemed to enjoy wearing it, probably in large part because he was often complimented on his attire. While I have no idea which kind of party Cajun preferred—birthday parties, memorial services, weddings, Bar Mitzvahs—it is my guess that he loved them all.

One party in particular proved to be an outstanding event for Cajun. The wedding occurred on August 19, 2010, and a couple named Twin and Erik Hagberg were the bride and groom. We knew the parents of the groom, Pat and Carl, but did not know his son nor his fiancée, Twin, who happens to be a genuine Polynesian princess. And while we were not on the guest list, the parents—who are extraordinarily generous and fun-loving people— told us that we should stop by when the party got underway.

The wedding promised to be unique, given the bride's Polynesian heritage, and the co-mingling of her traditions with the groom's New York City culture. The ceremony would take place in the late afternoon, and a dinner and party was scheduled to follow. Since the groom's family have owned a home in Truro for decades they are considered to be summer locals (in Truro there are at least three population classifications: locals—also known as natives, which I always thought was somewhat of a misnomer since they are not descendants of the true Native American natives, but rather are people whose families have lived in Truro for generations;

the washashores, who are people who were not born in Truro but now reside there; and the summer residents).

Since Pat and Carl Hagberg have spent many summers in Truro, enjoy entertaining, and are members of the PHYTC, they know people in the area from all walks of life, so the wedding party would be drawing a large, interesting, and unique crowd. Amidst it all, there was Cajun, who was always nonjudgmental and took to any large, interesting, and unique crowd as long as it came with food, music, love, and friendly people.

Before the Hagberg wedding party began, the band and caterers arrived to set up for the event. Cajun saw the party trucks arrive, and watched as a number of men began to set up the tent, chairs, tables, tablecloths, and place settings. He was on high alert, excited that something was going to happen soon. As finally the wedding guests arrived later in the afternoon, Cajun was out the door and on his way to do his meet and greet, wearing his black bowtie which we felt would be appropriate for this Polynesian-American wedding. Unlike most weddings, however, the guests arrived wearing colorful Polynesian and

Hawaiian shirts, white pants, flowered dresses, beads, flowers in their hair, and sandals. The wedding party—some who had come all the way from Polynesia—wore bright blue and white short-sleeved shirts with white pants for the men, and bright blue and white summer dresses for the women.

Cajun should have had an orchid attached to his collar, but we hadn't thought that far ahead. It was a beautiful day, and not a cloud in the sky.

The wedding ceremony would be held outside, on the white sand alongside the Pamet River, with the striking lime green marsh grass as a backdrop. The ceremony was performed by a non-denominational minister, and the gorgeous bride, Twin, wore a magnificently colored headdress, adorned with white beads that hung before her face in an appropriate style for a Polynesian princess. The handsome and happy groom, Erik, wore a blue and white Hawaiian type shirt and white pants.

Once the vows were said and the ceremony was over, the party began in earnest. Cajun, who had patiently sat in attendance with the other guests, was more than ready to get this party started! It wasn't long before the children, who were very much a part of the event, realized that entertaining Cajun and being entertained by him was more fun than mixing with the adults—and while some dogs are shy or don't trust children, Cajun adored them. He loved the attention, the petting, the kisses, the laughs, and the giggles. He was more than willing to take part in almost any activity the children were doing—save for playing fetch—and once the kids understood that this yellow dog wasn't going to chase after thrown objects, they found other ways to play with him. They stuck flowers in his collar, crawled under tables together, ran along the shoreline with him, and then finally had him join in with everyone on the dance floor.

Since this was a multi-cultural wedding, the music and dancing reflected that mix. Twin, and her friends and family, performed traditional dances—with everyone else attempting to follow along—and this was mixed together with westernized dancing. Cajun was naturally indiscriminate about dance forms, too, and joined in with the children in whatever way they could get him to move his paws to the beat. Soon they discovered that Cajun not only allowed them to spin him on his back on the dance floor, but he rather enjoyed it. . . as did everyone else watching since rarely has a wedding involved a dog spinning in the middle of a dance floor. Cajun loved it all, and anything he lacked in grace he made up for in attitude.

Everyone was happy—the way people usually are at weddings—enjoying friends, new family, a new husband and wife, and in this case the canine wedding crasher. When the party finally wound down and it was time to leave, Cajun was as disappointed as anyone to see it end. One by one the tired children came by to give him a hug or a kiss and say goodbye, and he watched forlornly as they got in their cars and drove away.

We stood with him in the parking lot and watched as the last of the headlights disappeared down the dirt road.

"The party's over, Cajun. We have to go home," I told my dejected dog. "There will be another wedding soon. I promise." But he looked so sad... it was obvious how much he'd loved this wedding. For dogs, the future does not exist; it is only the present that matters, and this wedding meant the world to Cajun, and he hadn't wanted it to end.

That night Cajun lay at the foot of our bed, snored heavily, and had not one nightmare. It had indeed been a great wedding.

And even if the future might not exist for him, he could always relive this past.

CHAPTER ELEVEN

Harbor Mayor

Since over two-thirds of Truro is National Seashore, most people today are attracted to the area because of its miles and miles of ocean and bay beaches, its hundred and fifty foot high dunes, its fresh water ponds and salt water inlets and estuaries, and its lack of visibility, glitz, and noise. In past centuries, the focal point within the town was its harbor. The Pamet Harbor is on a tidal river that flows from the Cape Cod Bay and winds westward through salt water marshes for a few miles; eventually it comes within a hundred yards of connecting with the Atlantic Ocean.

In the 1800's, the Pamet Harbor became a fairly prominent fishing port, with fish processing sheds, shipbuilding yards, grinding mills, windmills, three wharves for the many shipping vessels, a lighthouse, and a schooner that took passengers from Truro to Boston and back. However, the extreme tidal flow of the river and the constant silting in which the tides ebb and flow make it difficult to maintain the harbor as a navigable waterway. The water depth varies by ten feet or more throughout the day, meaning that the river at mean high tide might measure about twelve feet, but at low tide measures only about two feet. Dredging of the river has been done many times throughout the years, highlighting a constant battle against nature; this is the major reason the harbor is limited to smaller boats, which can more easily navigate the shifting sands.

Nevertheless, the harbor still maintains its prominence as a focal point for the town of Truro. Local fishermen come and go at all hours of the day and night to load and unload their boats with their catch, while others come to put boats in the water for a day trip or check on their moored boats.

Many people visit the harbor to kayak or canoe, and more simply watch the activity at the pier or the sun set in the evening sky. In other words, the Pamet Harbor is indeed a busy spot from the beginning of June until late September, and though Cajun's evenings were frequently occupied with party events, his daytime hours were relatively free—which allowed for visits to the Harbor-Master's shack and the pier.

The job of Harbor Master is not an easy one. It requires knowledge about the rules and regulations associated with boating and fishing, and the acuity of knowing when safety is at risk; but it also requires the ability to smoothly, effectively, and amicably work with sometimes adverse situations given the conflicts that inevitably arise.

In Truro there is one Harbor Master and at least two assistants who take on this job. Fortunately for Cajun, all of the people who have worked at the harbor—even amongst the different harbor masters and assistants over the years—have liked dogs.

In addition to the harbor masters and their assistants, there was one wonderful, fascinating, and kind gentleman who spent a good deal of time at the harbor. He went by "Uncle Al". Uncle Al did not work at the harbor, neither was he my uncle nor the Harbor Master's uncle. Uncle Al was Russell Zawaduck's uncle.

Russell—who happens to be a licensed boat captain and the owner of the charter fishing business called "Chasin' Tails"—lives down by the harbor with his family.

The Zawaducks are locals. Russell and his wife, Lisa, were born and raised in Provincetown, and bought property next to the Pamet Harbor and built a house there. Russell's uncle came to live with the family some years ago; he quickly became known as Uncle Al to everyone.

Uncle Al was always extremely affable, bright, well informed and up to date on the worldwide financial markets and current news events. Uncle Al also happened to be the person in the Zawaduck family who took care of their yellow Labrador Retriever, Tucker.

Uncle Al walked Tucker five or six times a day, fed him, bathed him, gave him extra treats, and made veterinary appointments when necessary. Uncle Al and Tucker were, during those years, best friends and great companions. On most days, after their walks, Uncle Al enjoyed taking Tucker down to the Harbor Master's shack to visit with whomever happened to be there.

Conversation was and is easy to come by at the shack, as town gossip and opinions on any and every subject get tossed about. Everyone who frequents the harbor knew Uncle Al, and most at least took a moment to stop and say hello. Tucker too clearly enjoyed hanging out at the harbor, where dog biscuits and friendly scratches behind the ears were plentiful.

It didn't take long for Cajun to discover the harbor group and endear himself to this cast of characters—Tucker, Uncle Al, the Harbor Master and assistants, boaters and kayakers, and pretty much anyone else who came to the harbor.

Soon after Uncle Al made the move to Truro, we happily became the beneficiaries of Uncle Al's broad knowledge and well thought out counsel, which ranged from financial stock market advice to the best place to buy bird seed, the problems with local weather forecasts, which newspaper carried the most reliable storm predictions, the best veterinarian to frequent, problems with canine skin rashes, where to purchase the cheapest dog biscuits, the most waterproof lightweight jackets, the quality or lack thereof of the repaving of the harbor parking lot, who to hire to dig the best well, the best car value, and when and how to water certain plants.

Cajun hung out with Uncle Al and Tucker in the early mornings or late afternoons, and frequently strolled on down to the harbor to see what might be going on there. Soon he realized that it was equally interesting to stroll down to the end of the pier and onto the ramp where the boats pull in and tie up in order to unload passengers, coolers, fishing gear, the catch of the day, lobster pots, and empty cans of gasoline. It was not uncommon to see Cajun sitting on the pier greeting fishermen as they took off for a day on the water or returned to dock, tie up, and unload their wares.

Cajun monitored all harbor activity, and was a neutral harbor overseer—he didn't care if someone owned a new $450,000, thirty-seven foot Boston Whaler 370 Outrage, a used $150 dinghy, an inflatable excursion, a canoe, a kayak, or a sunfish, and almost every boat-person greeted him or gave him a scratch behind the ear after they moored.

The time he spent at the end of the pier seemed to be a time of contemplation. He had no desire to jump in the water and take a swim. He had no desire to hop in one of the boats, though he was invited a number of times. More than one Harbor Master, and more than a few boat captains, suggested that if there were a position called "Mayor of the Pier" or "Harbor Mayor", Cajun could have proudly worn it.

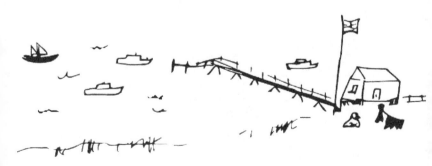

As the Elizabethan dramatist Thomas Dekker wrote in *The Shoemaker's Holiday*, "It's a mad life to be a lord mayor; it's a stirring life, a fine life, a velvet life, a careful life." I believe that is a fairly accurate reading of how Cajun might have characterized his mayoral position at the harbor.

It was stirringly emotional for us to watch this yellow dog, refugee from the floods of Hurricane Katrina and once on the verge of dying, now transformed; our boy was obviously pleased with life, and at peace "sitting on the dock of the bay", dutifully welcoming and receiving boaters, and wishing well to all fishermen as they embarked or disembarked on their daily excursions.

CHAPTER TWELVE

The Nor'easter

A nor'easter (also called a northeaster) is a storm that travels from the south (usually from the Gulf of Mexico) up the eastern seaboard and to the northeast, though actually the winds of such a storm originate in the north Atlantic coast of Canada or the Northeastern United States. Nor'easters are characterized by torrential rainfall, coastal flooding, high winds, lightning, thunder, dark clouds, large waves of ten feet or more, and significant beach erosion. And while they are most likely to hit between October and April, they can and do occur at any time of the year.

One year such a storm hit Cape Cod in mid-June. Uncle Al cautioned me about the coming storm as he relayed the local and national weather forecasts, some of which I had heard, and others he seemed to have a special private line on. The predictions called for heavy downpours that would last for a couple of days, with peak winds exceeding 75 mph; most worrisome to the fishermen was that the heaviest rainfall and highest winds might arrive during the high tide.

Moreover, Uncle Al warned, since the storm was going to hit when the moon was near full, the mean high tide would be higher than usual.

Uncle Al: "Gonna come in with a heavy hand."

Me: "Is that right?"

Uncle Al: "Yup. You bet. And if the wind gusts hit during the high tide, you're gonna see some flooding right over into the parking lot. Best hope it doesn't come near your cottage."

Me (worried now): "You think it will flood up to my place?"

Uncle Al: "Could. Yup, very well could."

Me: "Have you ever seen it flood that high?"

Uncle Al: "Almost. Yup... almost, though not quite. Better be that you hope for almost."

Me: "Almost, but not right up to the cottage...
right?"

Uncle Al: "Almost. You get winds that are close
to being as high as a hurricane... well, it can cause a
piece of damage... I'll say that much."

Me: "Well, what do you think will happen?"

Uncle Al: "I've got to watch the temperature differences. The greater the temperature differences between that low pressure coming up from the south and
that jet stream in the northeast—that will tell you just
how bad it's gonna be. The greater those differences,
then the angrier the storm when it arrives here."

Me: "Right. I understand. Hope it isn't bad."

Uncle Al: "Me too. Me too. But you know these
storms... they can just fall apart before they even get
here; and then again, they can intensify and get a
whole lot stronger than they are predicting. One
thing about a storm... nor'easter or a hurricane... the
weather people can only tell so much about what's
really going to happen. Only so much. What happens will happen. That's the truth of it."

Me: "Yes, your right. That's the truth of it. We'll
batten down the hatches and get ready. We'll surely
lose electricity."

Uncle Al: "Surely will lose the electric first thing. Russell's out bringing in the boats now. Most everybody is gonna bring 'em in, but some just tie 'em down and double anchor 'em and hope the boats can ride out the storm. I've seen more than a few get thrown up ashore during one of these storms. Fools are the men that don't bring their boats in... fools and gamblers. My mother always said gamblers were idiots, but then she was a tough Maine woman... you know those women from Maine are a different breed."

Me: "My grandfather was from Maine. Large, tough family. Eight kids."

Uncle Al: "Is that right? I figured you must have some tough in you. Maine tough. Good to know."

Me: "I figured you would like to know that. What does Tucker think of these storms?"

Uncle Al: "He doesn't care. He just curls up under the table and goes to sleep."

Me: "He's not bothered by thunder or lightning or winds or heavy rains?"

Uncle Al: "Not a piece. I don't know if that makes him smart or dumb... it's just how he is."

Me: "Not so much Cajun. He hates storms.

Hates when the wind howls and the rain pours, and he is petrified of the thunder and lightning."

Uncle Al: "Ever tried Rock Rose? Or Phosphorus?"

Me: "Rock Rose? Phosphorus?"

Uncle Al: "Don't know but I've heard people say they give that to a scared dog and it can calm him down. Don't know. Tucker just sleeps through it, like I said. You know what they say?"

Me: "No, what do they say?"

Uncle Al: "That there really isn't any cure for fear."

Me: "That's the truth... and, unfortunately for Cajun, it also has been said that fear has many eyes."

Hours before the storm was expected to hit we made preparations: got the lanterns and candles out, taped the windows, pulled the kayaks in and tied them close to the side of the house, took down the bird feeders, turned over the outside table, brought in the chairs, tucked the hanging plants in a safe place, filled the car's gas tank, filled jugs of water, filled the bathtub with water, stocked up on dry foods, and got the Monopoly and Scrabble games out. We were set.

Cajun was not, and Rousseau and Lucy didn't care one way or the other. They would watch Cajun's mental lapses, his panting and shaking, as something that was simply a part of his nature—they never seemed to judge him for it—just simply allowed that this was who he was.

I find dogs are extraordinary in that way; rarely do they make judgments, and not because they couldn't, but because they see no need to. While they might judge a vicious dog to be a danger or a threat, they do not judge a dog that has certain fears, or is obsessive in certain ways, to be any less of a dog. A dog can still enjoy the company of another dog that might actually be a bit odd.

A dog of limited intelligence is not seen by another dog as unworthy of friendship or acquaintanceship. Size is not an issue for dogs, nor is appearance: a big dog is not better than a small dog—simply bigger—and a groomed beauty is not better than a stinky, matted mess of a dog.

On the morning that The Storm was about to roll in, we awoke to a sky that was steely gray. The sun shone through the colorless wash like a white splatter of paint dropped onto a gray canvas. Down by the harbor we could see the birds frenetically in search of a meal before the storm hit— the gulls screeched their high pitched calls, and the plovers and terns swooped into the water looking for a morsel. The cormorants spread their splendid black wings and flitted from mooring to mooring, carefully watching for shadows to appear in the water.

Even the red-tailed squirrel that lives in the spruce tree beside our house was more brazen than usual, scurrying around tree trunks in search of seeds.

By mid-morning the weatherman on the local news station had updated the storm and announced that it would hit at 2:00 P.M, the winds would gust as high as 80 mph, precipitating high waves, potential beach erosion, and tree and property damage.

Before the storm hit we decided to head over to the ocean to see how ferocious the surf had become. The tide was coming in. High tide was scheduled for 3:04 p.m. that day, an hour after the storm was set to make landfall. The sky was growing darker and a thin mist was beginning to fall. Cajun was clearly aware that something troublesome was coming. After arriving at the beach parking lot, we slowly walked up a path that led to the top of a dune overlooking the Atlantic Ocean. The sound of the waves crashing against the dune's edge grew louder. When we finally reached the top, we were awestruck by the magnificence that stretched before us. Immense green-gray waves built upon one another, then crested with white foam thrusting upward and backward, one after the next breaking with a violent, resounding crash.

Streaks of foam sprayed sideways, bubbling and dancing off the backs of the breaking waves. The waves were massive, maybe 15 feet high, and there was no tide line. There was no shoreline. Each wave created a new tide line as one wave after the next reached the foot of the dunes and grabbed the sand, eroding what had been there for eons, taking it and swallowing it back into the sea.

There was no beach, at least not a beach a person or a dog or a crab or a seabird or a lone fox could wander along. It had been swallowed whole by a threatening and immensely angry ocean. The path that had once led down to the beach where, on a nice day, people would set up umbrellas and beach chairs, towels and coolers, had disappeared. We pulled our sweatshirt hoods up to stay somewhat dry.

The dogs were unconcerned about being soaked, they simply stared with fascination at the ominous sea. Lucy placed herself at Mark's feet, and Rousseau and Cajun sat side-by-side, staring out at the seething ocean.

We stayed for close to an hour, mesmerized by mother nature's invincible, unyielding strength. While only twenty-four hours before we had run through placid tidal pools and body-surfed gentle waves, now we wouldn't dare approach this wildly churning sea.

Once we were thoroughly soaked by the mist and the sea spray, we decided to head back home. The dogs were more than happy to leave, and though they hadn't done much physically, once we got them toweled off and inside the cottage, all three were exhausted from the outing.

At almost precisely 2:00 p.m., the winds picked up, the trees creaked and bent, and the beach grass bowed and danced. The wind was not continuous, rather it did what the weatherman said it would do—it gusted. The wind blew and then let up, blew harder and then let up again, and so too the beach grass and the limbs of the trees and the Rosa Rogosa bushes that thrive along sandy shorelines, and anything that was not tied down or nailed in or taped up or tucked under was orchestrated in a dance of its own by the punishing wind.

The window shutters rattled, a few shingles from someone's house blew through the grass, and an aluminum beach chair that had been left down by the Harbor Master's shack now bobbed in the water near the end of the pier.

The storm flag had been raised. Not the red triangle advising small craft warnings, not the double red triangles meant for gale warnings, but the storm warning flag—the square red flag with a black rectangle in the center—the one that is flown when the expected winds might exceed 55 mph. The lone square flag flapped and snapped as the wind gusts toyed with it. A chain that was loose on the flag pole banged back and forth, making a racket.

The storm had officially arrived, and the usually calm river inlet of the Pamet River was now anything but calm.

White caps peaked to create two to three foot waves, which for the river is a large wave. High tide would arrive in another forty-five minutes, but already the water was climbing far higher than the usual mean high tide. Waves broke onto the stairs that led from the beach below the pier up to the Harbor Master's shack, and water flooded into the parking lot.

During a typical high tide the marshes are completely flooded and the water reaches up onto the nearby sand dunes; during a typical low tide the water recedes, the stalks of sea grass stand six or seven feet tall, and the sandbars stretch for a mile or more out into the Cape Cod Bay.

During a storm, flooding can easily occur, particularly during a high tide, as the water rises above the harbor docks and the piers and completely floods the inland marshes, flowing over the dunes and onto the roadways and under house foundations.

My cottage is only 75 yards from the water's edge, and at best 35 feet above mean high tide. As I watched the waves break over the stairs next to the Harbor Master's shack and flow into the parking lot, as the wind gusts slapped against the side of the house, the screens on the porch bent inward, and the hinges on the porch door groaned, I most definitely worried.

And as the wind began to howl and the trees bent and the screen door hinges rattled, Cajun began to unravel. The final insult to his mental stability came about when the sky grew extremely dark and loud claps of thunder could be heard in the distance, and then lightning strikes flashed across the darkened skies.

Within minutes the rains arrived in buckets. The rain didn't pitter-patter against the rooftop, it splashed and clapped and pounded. Rainwater gushed over the edges of the flooded gutters and ran down the window panes. Then there was more thunder and more streaks of white lightning. The sky lit up for a few seconds.

Then more thunder. And more lightning.

Cajun stared at the window, became wide eyed, and began to shake violently. His eyes darted from the window to Mark to me, and back again to the window. He panted and drooled. And then the lights went out. While hours before the storm had seemed exciting, now it was just an immense challenge to hope we didn't get flooded, to hope the house withstood the winds and rain, but mostly to get Cajun through the storm in any way possible.

Both of us got down on the floor with Cajun, stroked his back, rubbed his belly, scratched behind his ears and spoke calmly to him; but when a strong gust of wind blew against the porch door, unhinged the latch, and sent the door crashing backwards and slamming against the wall, Cajun completely came unglued. He could not stop shaking. With each thunder clap and every lightning strike he shook more violently.

We decided to put all three dogs in the car and just drive—anywhere.

As we headed down the road with the radio blasting classic rock to drown out the storm, the windshield wipers flapping back and forth on high speed, and doing our best to avoid the deepest of puddles and flooded roads, Cajun seemed to settle just a bit.

We took the back roads of Truro and headed towards Provincetown. Along the way, we passed numerous small summer cottages that usually would be booked with guests, but now appeared deserted. We

assumed that whoever had been staying in these cottages had packed up their beach chairs, umbrellas, towels, boogie boards, bathing suits, and flip flops and drove off the Cape across the exit bridges, the Sagamore or Bourne, and returned home to safety, electricity, and quiet.

We drove over to the Highland Lighthouse, which is situated atop a dune that rises almost 150 feet above the Atlantic Ocean. It was the first lighthouse built on Cape Cod in 1797 to help ships navigate the shifting sands, tricky shoals and shoreline along the outer Cape. We could see the light flashing through the pouring rain and thick fog, but it was no time to stop and watch—we had to keep moving to keep Cajun mollified. We turned the truck around and made our way over to a nearby beach, driving in circles around the large parking lot and assuring that the car wouldn't come to a halt. This allowed us to see the ocean, which was now in full-blown fury with green waves rising skyward, cresting and crashing upon each other as far as the eye could see.

It was hard to imagine anything having an easy time in the ocean that day, no matter if it were a whale or a bluefish, an oyster, lobster, or clam. I suspect that every living thing must have hunkered down as close to the floor of the ocean as possible.

I had heard that sometimes seabirds can get caught up in the eye of big storms and get taken hundreds of miles inland, only to have to find their way back or perish.

It was clear, however, that just the sight of the ocean was making Cajun nervous, so we drove into Provincetown and slowly navigated along the main drag, Commercial Street. We spotted a few people walking and dodging puddles, and in the windows of bars and restaurants that had lost electricity kerosene lanterns and candles had been lit to keep customers cozy and happy.

After meandering through Provincetown we decided to return home. The rain had finally begun to settle into a drizzle, and a few puffy white clouds formed against a backdrop of a gray skyline. We passed a boarded up pizza shop, one gas station that was open and another that was closed, and a few empty-looking motels.

It might as well have been mid-winter from the looks of things, as the outer Cape had become deserted.

The following morning the sky was a bright, clear blue. Looking out the bedroom window as the first rays of light appeared—around 4:45 a.m.—the harbor and the bay were once again calm. Not a crest nor a wave could be seen in the distance.

It was as if there had never been a storm the day before. The gulls, plovers, terns, and other seabirds had returned to squawk and cry and dive for food. Fishermen were backing their trucks down the ramp and putting their boats into the water again.

The red flag with the black rectangle in the center was gone and replaced with the large flapping American flag. It was just another day. I got up and took Cajun out for a morning run.

Nothing was said between us about the storm. He didn't mention it and neither did I.

CHAPTER THIRTEEN

And Then There Was the Time When...

In our family people come and go, appear and disappear from my home—except for the dogs and me. We are steady and stable, routine and dependable, a bit like the center of a wheel. And because the dogs and I are together so much of the time, we have come to understand and read one another quite well. And while unquestionably I have loved my dogs equally, I spent more time with Cajun because he liked and was capable of longer and harder hikes than the other two dogs who shared our home. Because of this, Cajun and I conversed more often and more regularly. Sometimes we spoke out loud to each other, but more often than not we communicated with smiles, frowns, nods, tail wags, tears, and the suchlike.

I always treated Cajun like a male dog because he was a male dog. I did not treat him like another person because he was not a person; and I don't think he would have appreciated being confused for a person, either. Cajun was fine with being a dog, and I believe he preferred being a dog over anything else. He quite liked to wander up the road sniffing and peeing on trees and bushes, and he truly enjoyed rubbing up against a snow-bank to scratch his sides, and he loved being scratched behind the ears and having his stomach rubbed.

He was not interested in driving the car—he wanted to be chauffeured. He enjoyed hanging his head out of the window of the back passenger seat, so that the people in cars alongside could smile and say hello to him, and he particularly liked sticking his head out the window when the car was parked so that people passing by could compliment, take his picture, pat his head, and tell him how handsome he was.

He liked doing things I would not imagine many people would have enjoyed doing because he was an extraordinarily sweet, loyal though independent, amusing though serious, proud male dog.

As for Cajun's treatment of me—well, he always treated me as his best friend, a person, not as another dog. He expected me to use my hands to make him his meals each day and fill his water bowl to the brim. He, like all dogs I've known, loved belly rubs, treats, and bones from the butcher. When I would confide in him various things that were on my mind he tried valiantly to understand what I was saying, but was not particularly concerned if he did not. Most importantly, he understood the gravity of what I was saying by reading my emotions and moods. He knew when I was sad, happy, angry, mellow, or excited.

Cajun always kept one eye on me, evaluating my every expression. Correctly. Cajun knew me. We were the very best of friends: "A friend is a person with whom I may be sincere. Before him, I may think aloud."—Ralph Waldo Emerson So one day, when my mind was particularly swirling with unresolved issues, questionable plans, decisions that seemed important at the time (though probably were not), I set off on a hike with Cajun along a trail called Difficult—it was one we frequently hiked. It was autumn. The colors were changing, the mountainsides had turned from vibrant green to brilliant gold and orange, the bears were hungrily and actively foraging before winter's hibernation, the elk were rutting and the deer were mating; coyotes, foxes, squirrels, hares, and all other wildlife were busy preparing for winter. Cajun and I hiked many miles up the narrow and steep terrain that morning, through groves of canopy-covered, gold-leafed Aspen trees. My mind was noisily spinning in that muted fashion that seems private, when Cajun, who was ahead of me on the path, stopped, turned around and stared at me.

"What?" I asked. He simply stared. "What?" I said again. Cajun stood his ground.

"So... ? You can hear my mind spinning? Is that it?" His head tilted slightly to the side.

"Okay, so you're saying I need to drop it, get into the moment, right?"

Cajun stared at me, shook all over, clearly (at least I thought so) telling me to lose the OCD head spin, and then he turned and headed back up the trail. He had made his point.

The beginning of the Difficult Trail is 8,140 feet in altitude and at the end it is about 9,500 feet. It isn't a terribly hard trail to climb, its name aside, as it leads into the Collegiate Peaks Wilderness area, winding through tall thick aspen groves and spruce trees, sometimes following alongside Difficult Creek, sometimes veering away from it. At certain points on the trail a person can look to the west and see below the snakelike winding Roaring Fork River as it runs through the valley; and then, if one turns eastward there is the view of the 12,000 foot peaks surrounding Independence Pass.

After a few miles there is a bend in the trail that leads into a thick forest of spruce and aspen trees. Difficult Creek runs alongside it, and a posted sign reads: "Trail not maintained beyond this point." Cajun and I passed the sign— because it is what we liked to do—and found ourselves climbing over boulders and fallen trees.

"This is the best part, isn't it?" I said to Cajun. He agreed.

After another quarter of a mile we both stopped. I sat down on a patch of brush along the side of the creek, and Cajun sat next to me. It was time for a break. I gave Cajun a couple of treats, and then retrieved my own treat and water. "It's a good day, isn't it?"

Cajun agreed.

And then Cajun's nose twitched, and he was clearly alerted that something was nearby.

"What is it?" I asked.

A few moments later a tall, thin, gray and white coyote trotted out from the thick brush. Clearly he hadn't expected to see us sitting on the side of "his" path. The coyote stopped dead in his tracks and stared at us. Cajun stood absolutely still and stared back. I, too, was frozen on the spot.

I have seen coyotes many times before, but usually when they see a person or a dog larger than a beagle, they take off. Coyotes are shy. They rarely attack unless they are looking at small prey. Confronting an adult or a fair-sized dog is not an opportune situation for a coyote—they cannot risk being seriously injured, and it doesn't seem worth their while to take on a human or a mid-sized dog and possibly lose the fight.

This coyote, however, seemed so surprised to see us that rather than taking off he just stood his ground. Cajun began to bare his teeth and growl. I had never seen him do that before.

"Hey buddy," I soothed. "Take it easy. Don't start anything. Let's just hope this guy moves along."

The coyote continued to stand his ground. He stared at me and then at Cajun. His yellow eyes didn't signify either anger or fear—if anything he simply seemed curious.

Cajun continued growling, which is when two more coyotes appeared from behind the brush.

"Damn. Settle down, Cajun. This is not a fight we want to start. Don't move an inch," I advised Cajun, while firmly holding onto his collar. I figured they wanted Cajun to bolt so that then they could take him down. We sat and nervously waited for the pack to make their decision, as I scanned the ground, looking for rocks or sticks to use as defense if need be.

Cajun continued to stare at the pack. I warned him not to growl, not to threaten them, just to stay still. "Settle. Stay quiet. Remain cool," I repeated softly.

Minutes passed. The coyotes stared at us. Cajun stared at them. I tried to avoid looking them in the eye. Who was the most nervous? Without a doubt it was me, but after a long stretch of what was probably only minutes—but seemed much longer—the coyotes turned and trotted off into the thicket of trees.

"Damn," I said, shaken.

Cajun sniffed the air, stared into the woods where the coyotes had disappeared.

"That definitely put my mind back into the moment." I said, resting my head on Cajun's neck.

Cajun turned and licked my face. "Let's go home."

And so we headed down the trail.

And then there was another time when...

Cajun took one of his commonplace afternoon strolls around the neighborhood, walked down the recently plowed driveway of a fairly new two-story house, climbed up the entry steps, and—realizing that the front door was ajar—let himself in. He then proceeded to saunter up the carpeted stairs to the second floor, heard someone in one of the rooms, ambled in, and was greeted by the homeowner, who was soaking in his bathtub.

Fortunately for Cajun, the gentleman in the bathtub is an extremely thoughtful man, who fortu-itously happens to like dogs. Cajun, feeling no sense of embarrassment or shame at invading a stranger's bathroom while that stranger was taking a bath in the privacy (theoretical privacy) of his home, mo-seyed up to the tub and sat down next to it.

"Hey." The nice man said, going with the moment.

And for the next twenty minutes, Cajun sat be-side the man in the tub while they conversed.

The nice gentleman's wife also thought the sit-uation was humorous, and politely telephoned me to say that Cajun had paid them a visit, just in case I was wondering where he was. Opportunely, the family (there are also two sons) did not have any dogs at the time, and once they had been introduced to Cajun, decided they wanted a dog of similar temperament and looks. After much research, they found a wonderful yellow lab that looked a bit like Cajun, named her Gracie, and then soon thereafter decided one was not enough. They found another similar-looking yellow lab, named her Rose, and our neighborhood began to look a little bit dog-cloned.

And then there was the time when...

While in Truro during the summer months, Mark and I decided that when we went to the beach we should bring not just one umbrella, but two. One for us, Rousseau, and Lucy and a second, OF COURSE, for Cajun. Why? Because Cajun liked to lie on his back, in the shade, under the umbrella, which always took up too much room and did not allow for anyone else—human or animal—to enjoy the shade.

So two umbrellas it was, which was a bit of a nuisance since the dogs carried none of their own beach necessities, and we typically walked across a fairly steep dune to get to our quiet spot.

Cajun, however, rarely followed us across the dune to our spot. No, Cajun liked to take a different route, which took him a few hundred yards down a dirt road, which in turn led to the public beach access path, which in turn allowed him to stroll past whoever might be set up on the beach.

This gave him his opportunity to greet his fellow beachgoers, sit with them under their umbrella, hang out with them on a shared towel, and enjoy being talked to and petted by his newfound friends. In fact, Cajun met many of his friends this way—people neither Mark nor I knew—and one Canadian trio in particular became quite good friends with Cajun. This occasioned us to become friends with them soon thereafter, too. Clearly country of origin never mattered to Cajun—nor height, weight, age, accent, race, religion. If they were good people, he was their good friend.

And indeed the Canadians were very good people, the daughter taking enough pictures of Cajun that she could use one as her screensaver and introduce Cajun by photo to her friends, which naturally increased his worldly status as a very fine dog.

And then there was the time when...

Cajun decided a massage might be good to try when he wandered over to the Aspen Club, which at the time boasted outdoor and indoor tennis, squash, racquetball, an Olympic-size swimming pool, saunas, jacuzzis, a complete fitness, yoga, and workout center, and a fine massage and treatment spa.

In order to enter the massage spa, one had to go through double doors, which Cajun accomplished (though no one seemed to know quite how), and into the waiting room with its inviting couches, chairs and fireplace. Cajun, as I was told, made himself at home in the waiting area with the guests who awaited their appointments, making friends as was his custom. It didn't take long before a massage therapist decided there was no reason not to offer Cajun a massage, too, since he seemed to have been such a polite and patient guest while in the waiting room. The fact that he might not tip as well as the other guests never crossed the mind of his therapist, and so he obliged Cajun with a nice rubdown, spine massage, fore and hind legs massage, and ear and neck treatment.

Cajun spent well over an hour at the Aspen Club Spa, and would probably have stayed longer if one of the guests hadn't thought this yellow dog might be lost and telephoned me. When I picked Cajun up some fifteen or so minutes later he was not ecstatic to see me, though he was decidedly relaxed and happy.

And then there were so many other times... too many to recount.

CHAPTER FOURTEEN

Loving All of Him

When Cajun came into my life, his will to survive was unquestionably strong but I don't believe that was exactly what enabled him to blossom into the dog he would become. When we first brought him home, he wanted to live—he just didn't know how or why he wanted to live—but he knew that he wanted to survive. Most creatures would choose life over death, so that in and of itself is not particularly unusual; but in the face of everything he had seen, heard, smelled, and survived, his desire was shaken by his reality.

He was fragile. He had lost trust in the world around him, he had lost trust in the skies, in the wind, in the roll of thunder, in people, in other dogs, in anything out of the ordinary. His world had been shattered, and yet he still wanted to believe that the moment before him would be better than the moment behind. And, fortunately for him, that turned out to be true.

It was not at all easy to watch Cajun when he became unhinged, but it was a gift to be a part of his newfound delight in life. He became the dog he needed to be with all his bumps, bruises and edges: a dog with a great heart, a deep soul, a willful nature, a vulnerable spirit, an intense belief in the moment, a ridiculous sense of humor, and most importantly, an unabashed excitement for each day to begin. That last one was a gift in itself.

Cajun looked to me for love, security, and care. And I looked to him as my most loyal and very best confidant and friend, and the one who would always remind me to stay in the moment when I tended to obsess too much over the past or the future.

Without a doubt he was as important to me as I was to him.

When, at the age of sixteen Cajun's health and strength began to falter, I went into partial, though not full-blown, denial. In the fall of 2017 it was clear that he couldn't hike as far—so we went for slow, short walks which he still enjoyed. It was during this time that I had shoulder replacement surgery, which meant less exercise and more nap time for me, too.

Cajun liked that I spent hours on a Lazy Boy recliner icing my shoulder and watching television. He lay at my side, and together we watched every U.S. Open tennis match, though given the number of pain killers I was taking, I could probably recall what happened in those matches about as well as Cajun did.

And when the finals of both the women's and men's U.S. Open had ended, Cajun and I binge-watched Netflix's Nurse Jackie, and when that was finished we honed in on the first episodes of Schitt's Creek. Without a doubt Cajun enjoyed me staying in one place, my switch to an easy-going lifestyle, and my half-doped laughter and enjoyment of these shows.

But as I slowly began to heal, Cajun did not.

He developed what is called Laryngeal Paralysis, or Lar Par. Lar Par is a disease of the cartilage of the larynx. While normally the function of the larynx is to close after one exhales and then open when one inhales—completely shutting during eating or drinking—for an animal with Lar Par this does not happen.

Breathing is labored and exceedingly difficult; the affected dog gasps for air, pants or coughs, and suffocation is a possibility. Lar Par commonly affects older and larger breed dogs, and is extremely stressful for dogs, who obviously do not understand what is going on. They become despondent and exhausted by the struggle to breathe.

Though surgery can be successful, it is not usually recommended for a sixteen-year-old dog. I sought the advice of my veterinarian and friend, Scott Dolginow, who had known Cajun since his adoption many years ago. Scott, who cares far more for dogs than people, and who donates weeks each year to spay programs in Mexico and adopts three-legged and blind dogs without hesitation, also understood my deep attachment and love for Cajun.

We had discussed Cajun's aging and health many times before the Lar Par diagnosis, and while Scott has successfully operated on a number of dogs with the condition, he also pointed out that Cajun's health had become compromised. His hind quarters were weak, he had difficulty getting up, was no longer able to traverse stairs, and even frequently fell during the simple act of walking.

Cajun had become confused, and though I vehemently disagreed with Scott about his suggestion that Cajun suffered from dementia, that too was probably setting in.

He had also become incontinent, and I was having to clean up after him two or three or four times a day. I did it without question, considering it to be a minor problem, though I knew that Cajun was clearly not happy about his incontinence—his dignity suffered.

I tried to convince Cajun that it was okay, and that the inability to negotiate the stairs was okay, and that falling was not so terrible, but after months of watching Cajun decline it became abundantly apparent to me that he was depressed and anxious.

His coughing became so violent on some nights that he would throw his head against the floor in order to try to catch a breath. I could not bear the idea of Cajun suffocating —a horrible death—but stubbornly and mistakenly I hoped and prayed that he would get better.

At this point in Cajun's life both Rousseau and Lucy had passed away, and I had adopted another

mini long-haired dachshund from a puppy mill rescue and named him Yazhi (which my youngest son,
who speaks a bit of Navajo, told me means "the little
one"). I had also adopted a white English golden
retriever. The golden came with the name Charlie,
which has morphed into various nicknames from
Cholo to Chaz to Sir Charles.

Both Yazhi and Charlie were devoted to Cajun,
who was eleven when they arrived in our household.
Cajun was the elder statesman, the savant when it
came to anything and everything in the neighborhood or on hikes; he was the gentle and thoughtful
leader of their pact.

As the years passed and Cajun at sixteen walked
slower, clearly weaker than he used to be, they became more attentive and loving, licking and kissing
and cuddling with him.

However, the coughing, heavy breathing, and
times of near suffocation disturbed Yazhi and Charlie almost as much as it distressed Mark and me.

During the last months of Cajun's life, Scott
tried to gently convince me that "it was time". Mark
and I discussed this as many as five-hundred times,
no exaggeration. Neither of us could convince our-

selves to do what we knew was probably the kindest thing for Cajun.

I, in particular, just could not let go. Selfish, yes. But I could not bring myself to put Cajun to sleep, and I was in emotional agony over the situation.

Then one night in May, Cajun became so distraught by not being able to catch a breath that he threw his head against the floor and almost knocked himself out. Mark and I lay on the floor with him. Loved him. Promised him that he would not have to go through this hell anymore.

I scheduled an appointment for the vet to come to the house. I canceled it.

A week later I scheduled another appointment. I canceled it.

Cajun became worse and worse. And again I promised him that I would not let him suffer.

I had to let him go.

He needed me to help him not suffer any longer. And on the morning I finally gave in to what most people would call reason, but I would call life's final cruel roadblock, I lay with him on the floor... and he went to sleep and passed away. I thanked him for just being himself. For all the gifts he had given me and had gifted to everyone he touched. For being the saint that he was. For being Cajun.

And letting him go? I was broken to the core.

Who ever knew that a dog could mean so much, become so important, be so integral, be so special, be so vital to his best friend? Cajun seemed to complete me in many ways, and I completed Cajun in all the other ways.

I know we might say this about the people we love the most, but I personally have never said that about any of my other dogs.

I miss Cajun every single day. And I always will. I love and have loved every dog I've adopted, but for me, forever and ever, there will never ever be another Cajun.

CHAPTER FIFTEEN

Memories

Cajun passed away in May of 2018. A few weeks later Mark, Yazhi, Charlie, and I loaded up and took off for another summer on Cape Cod. When we arrived at the Truro cottage after the annual trek across country—exhausted from the journey—Mark decided to wash the car and rid it of the bugs accumulated while driving through Colorado, Nebraska, Iowa, Illinois, Indiana, Ohio, Pennsylvania, New York, and Massachusetts. However, though the water worked perfectly fine inside the cottage, it didn't work at the outside hose. So I telephoned the plumber, who came out the very next day to fix it for us. After investigating the situation for about ten minutes he told us: "It's all fixed."

"That's terrific, thank you," I replied. "Yeah, pretty easy fix," he added.

"Really? What seemed to be the problem?" I asked.

"Ah. Well, the hose was kinked!" he laughed. "Just needed to be straightened on out."

"No way! That was all it was? Kinked?" I laughed, not wanting to out Mark as the one who missed such a small thing and cost us a plumber visit.

The plumber then turned to us and said, "Hey, by the way, do you recall a yellow lab-mix dog that used to live around here? Great dog. Four years ago my wife and I got married right over there at the Pamet Yacht Club," he said, pointing in the direction of the club. "And well, as we were standing at the altar, this yellow dog came up and sat right down at my feet. He didn't disturb us at all. Just sat next to me as if he were the best man... which he kind of was at that point!"

"Really?" I asked, knowing exactly who he was talking about.

"Yes," the plumber continued. "I remember now... he had a blue collar... his name was Cajun.

He spent the entire evening with us. At the wedding dinner and then he stuck around for the party after, too. He had a great time. Terrific dog. Everyone loved him! In fact, if you can believe it, Cajun is in all our wedding photos! Do you believe that?"

"Yes I do."

In Memory of Cajun

164

168

Acknowledgments

Cajun brought laughter and love, humility and reason to hundreds, if not thousands of people from many different countries. He was not worldly, but he had a sensibility that was engaging. So first and foremost, I want to thank Cajun – for this is his story and this was his gift.

I also wish to thank Seth Sachson, Bland Nesbit, and Ann Gurchick who, through the auspices of the Aspen Animal Shelter were able to reach out and help with the rescue efforts following the devastation of Hurricane Katrina, and bring needy dogs back to Aspen for fostering and sometimes adoption. Among those they rescued was one mess of a yellow dog and it was they who created the possibility for this dog to thrive and lead an incredible life.

I also wish to thank Dr. Scott Dolginow for helping to bring Cajun back to health from day one, and always being there for Cajun and me when either or both of us needed it.

I clearly want to thank Mark LeRose who loved Cajun unconditionally through trials and tribulations.

And I want to thank my three sons, Joe, Blue, and Nikos for always being there for me and for Cajun throughout.

Most importantly, I cannot say how very grateful I am in every way for the advice, support, and encouragement given by Michael Korda. I hold his counsel and recommendations in the highest regard. Thank you, Michael.

Additionally, I wish to acknowledge David Carriere who believed in this book early on and helped carry it through to completion.

And lastly, I wish to acknowledge all the people who gave Cajun more than a nod in life. They too contributed to his unique character, allowed him to come into their lives, allowed him to love them and offered him the same in return.

About the Author

BROOKE NEWMAN is an international, best-selling author and an award-winning playwright. Her previous titles, including the hugely successful THE LITTLE TERN (which was crafted into a play and made into a musical CD in Japan), and her critically acclaimed releases JENNIEMAE AND JAMES, ISSUES AND TRENDS IN HEALTH, and THE LOST TERN, have in total sold more than two million copies in seventeen countries worldwide. NOT ALWAYS HOME BEFORE DARK is the author's sixth published book. The mother of four adult children, the author resides in Aspen Colorado.